T0132283

A REASON FOR

Rainbows

PATRICIA CORNETT

BALBOA.PRESS

A DIVISION OF HAY HOUSE

Balboa Press books may be ordered through booksellers or by contacting:

Balboa Press
A Division of Hay House
1663 Liberty Drive
Bloomington, IN 47403
www.balboapress.com
1 (877) 407-4847

Scripture quotations marked WEB are taken from the World English Bible, public domain

Print information available on the last page.

ISBN: 978-1-9822-4333-3 (sc)
ISBN: 978-1-9822-4334-0 (hc)
ISBN: 978-1-9822-4332-6 (e)

Library of Congress Control Number: 2020905172

Balboa Press rev. date: 04/16/2020

DEDICATION

This book is dedicated
To the
Life and Memory of
My beloved son,
Jesse David Cornett.

CONTENTS

Dreams do come true, but when higher purposes than any the Dreamer envisions are infused into them, untold magnificent and unimaginable outcomes will inevitably unfold.

This powerful true story of love, courage, and thought-provoking revelations offers practical nutritional information, clinical research, and spiritual insights narrated from the perspective of a mother's love for her child so profound it sends her on a trek that starts out in a determined effort to learn ways to help him thrive, and turns into a journey in search of the purpose of life and what heaven is really all about.

ACKNOWLEDGEMENTS

It is said that time heals all things. I have observed, however, that it is really Love that heals, and Time acts as a substrate to assist the Divine Love's activity in ushering into our life the people, the conditions, and the experiences that work together to eventually reveal our renewed ability to smile again, to laugh again, and to dream again so that we are able to accomplish our life with dignity, with gratitude, with compassion, hope, and grace. And so, it is with deepest gratitude that I express my sincere thanks in recognizing not only those who have contributed to this book, but to the ones who have consistently encouraged me to "get this story out there." And there are others, as well.

To Valerie Hudson, you have my deepest gratitude and love for the friendship you have shown, for your encouragement, and for your extensive research on behalf of the entire CF population. The benefits in quality of life for the individual patient and for families can scarcely be quantified. Certainly, this is true for Jesse David and me.

To my brothers and sisters, John, Scott, Cheri, Tracey, Judy, Gina, Vincent, and Clinton, I have been aware of your unwavering support, and your recognition that I am forever changed by these profound experiences, and yet each of you have so willingly embraced the new me. And it is the loveliest thing to realize that I've never heard those all too well-meaning words, "it's time to move on." Certainly, I am moving, and I've always felt your enthusiastic support of every step I have taken in the process of healing and the renewing of my own confidence to achieve my life to its fullest capacity.

And to those who've given their unspoken permission, by listening with open heart and mind without reservation, for me to speak of Jesse David as if he were still here among us, I offer my heart-felt thanks. To me he is very much alive, not only in my memories and in my heart, but I believe the Intelligence that placed us here is more real and more alive than this ever-changing mortal plane that has, nevertheless, served us so well. Each of you, family, friends, and peers, have played an integral role in the healing of my heart, and I offer my blessings to you, and to the journey that has taken me from where I first began, and more than once I am sure, to where I Am now.

With all my Heart's Love,
Patricia Cornett, A Reason For Rainbows

FOREWORD

I knew, and yet did not know, Jesse Cornett. I never communicated with Jesse, even online, but as I learned more about his life in this poignant account by his mother Patricia, I came to a new understanding about what a special young man he was. But even more, I came to a new understanding of what a special woman Patricia is. For while I have never met Patricia Cornett in person, I know her heart.

Patricia's life intersected with mine for the first time in 2003, when she emailed me about her then-13 year old son Jesse. Three of my children have the disease Jesse had--cystic fibrosis--and I was trying to understand its pathophysiology well enough to help them. My family and I had appeared on the Today Show to talk about our efforts, and after her sister told Patricia about the show, she reached out to me. This is what she said in that very first email:

> Congratulations on the wonderful progress of your children and your courage and determination to excel as a mother of CF children.
>
> I say congratulations, because I always want to celebrate the triumphs of our efforts - those of us who are determined to do all we can so that our CF children can be and do all they can.

I am a full-time working mother of a 13 year old CF child, diagnosed at age 5, although I knew that we were facing something out of the "norm" from the time he was 3+ years old. Like you I have not accepted the fate the "specialists" prognosed for my son, and have done much research and made many strides on my son's behalf that have done great things for my son, Jesse David. At one point the doctors asked me "what are you doing right?" (17 June 2003)

Though back then we could not see what Journey lay in store for Jesse, I think you can understand why I felt so close to Patricia from this very first email. When I think of the word "determination," I think of Patricia Cornett, for she is the pure embodiment of that virtue. When I think of the word "loyal," I think of how loyal Patricia has always been to Jesse, standing by his side when others shrank from doing so—a loyalty that could never be interrupted by death. Indeed, the volume you hold in your hands is an eloquent testimony to that loyalty. Because of Patricia, Jesse's wise and beautiful spirit will continue to bring healing in our world.

Patricia was fearless in diving into the research literature; every week I would receive several emails summarizing the articles she had been reading, as well as hearing updates about how Jesse was doing. She was also fearless in advocating for the best care Jesse could receive, fearless in prodding the CFF by writing to them about new therapies, fearless in drafting a professional brief[i] on a treatment that still has great potential to help CF patients[ii] —in fact, a form of it is being used today in the coronavirus pandemic of 2020[iii].

As this book will share, Jesse passed away in October of 2006. My own daughter, who did not have CF, passed away suddenly in August of 2005, so I knew what Patricia was going through.

But she was much further along the path of understanding than I. She wrote to me soon after Jesse's death,

> God has been so compassionate to me. I keep getting a better and clearer recognition of His plan - that there IS a plan, one for each of us individually, which is itself an awesome thought, but what is way high and wonderful is that he's working each of us and the individual plan He has designed for us into the greater universal plan. Like a puzzle within a puzzle, a picture within a picture. (29 October 2006)

I am slowly seeing what Patricia saw. But maybe I can see something that Patricia cannot, and so I say it here in the foreword to this unforgettable volume: the kind of love that Patricia has for Jesse is a type of the love the Savior has for all of us. I feel that Patricia understands the heart of God more than most as a result because of how well, how loyally, how determinedly, and how unfailingly she loved her son. I can only guess at how much God loves Patricia for how she loved His son Jesse.

So while, yes, this book is Jesse's story, read it also for Patricia's story. Both Jesse and Patricia have gifts to give us, and both are precious beyond measure.

Valerie M. Hudson
April 2020

Valerie M. Hudson is a University Distinguished Professor and holds the George H.W. Bush Chair in the Department of International Affairs of The Bush School of Government and Public Service, Texas A&M University, where she directs the Program on Women, Peace, and Security.

[i] http://uvicf.org/researchnewsite/glutathionenewsite/GSNO.html
[ii] https://www.ncbi.nlm.nih.gov/pubmed/23523754
[iii] https://www.dailymail.co.uk/health/article-8197899/Could-nitric-oxide-treat-coronavirus-doctors-testing-gas-gave-Viagra.html

PREFACE

I began journaling a few weeks after Jesse David's transition in order to create an outlet and a means for stirring my soul and unlocking myself from the shock, sorrow, and dismay I felt over his passing. Jesse lived a mere sixteen and a half years with the life-shortening genetic disorder known as Cystic Fibrosis, yet he maintained a determination to survive. His confidence and compassion toward his own life and others can only be deemed uncommon by any standards.

I did not intend to write this book when I began journaling. The decision evolved as my observations of Jesse's life and our experiences began to formulate a positive message with a constructive force in my life. My foremost reason for putting this story in print is to bind my memories of the gift of Life and Love afforded me and entrusted to my care.

My notes-to-self of personal revelations and experiences, along with explanations and insights shared with others, helped me put the pieces of my life together anew and make sense of circumstances and outcomes well enough to survive emotionally.

Although the accounts of our experiences are precise in the pages that follow, they are by no means all-inclusive. And while I do not intend to draw sympathy or create sorrow, the story of Jesse's life, both written and unwritten, is nevertheless not meant for the weak of heart. That said, however, having observed him, having loved him, and loving him still, my personal interpretation of the purpose of Life has been ever more greatly magnified.

INTRODUCTION

I conclude that in the perfecting of our souls each of us constructs specific challenges, whether consciously or unconsciously, intended to build our eternal character and attain our individual mastery of life. Certainly, if this is true, then as for me I can think of no greater requirement than to have to return the one I have loved so deeply to the Source of the very Love that gifted me so magnificently. And as for you, my Beloved, I can think of no greater challenge than to give up every hope, every dream, and every desire for the sake of being perfected in all that you are eternally.

You always thought you were not strong, but I tell you I know the power of the Love that brought you to me, as if at my command. And I know the power of the Love that has led me from where I first began to where I am now. Your life, while you were here and since you have gone, has been the amazing miracle of God's Love manifest in my own life that continually draws me, convinces me, and raises me into the Heart of the mighty, loving Source of our existence.

You, Jessed David, remain my most studied teacher, my forerunner, my crown, and the greatest privilege of my life.

CHAPTER 1

An Explanation

IN THIS WORLD I BELIEVE FORGIVENESS is the axis upon which life must turn and that it is perhaps the greatest of the laws of Life provided to humanity. Once invoked, Forgiveness *will* act. It will heal conditions, and as it continues to gain momentum, it will release us into the greater and greater freedom of Life until we recall what we originally intended to do, which is simply to love.

When we begin to understand the magnificent power inherent in the activity of Forgiveness and then embrace it as a gift one would give to them self, we realize the recipient of our forgiveness actually experiences our intentions as a side effect, because we cannot send forth anything, whether it be word, thought, or deed, unless it exists within us, and therefore is already acting in our own life. With this in mind, it is my hope the story I share will be an encouragement, increasing hope through the greater understanding of the gifts of Life provided to everyone.

Thus, I begin.

FOR THE ROSES

"And you? When will you begin that long journey into yourself?" ~ *Rumi*

If asked when I first began my study of what defines real love, I would say the ripe old age of three or four years old. It was a perfect summer day as I recall. My parents, sisters, brothers and I were gathered in the front yard of our house. My father seemed to be having a pleasant time with us. He even decided to swing me by my arms in a circle around him, and at first it seemed I had never had so much fun. But after two or three rotations my instincts told me otherwise, and I knew I was headed for a painful disappointment. I called out to alert him that he was moving too close to the rose bushes lining the fence around our yard, but he would not hear me. I tried to break free of his hold, and when I could not break free, I coiled my legs as much as possible. Then, in what seemed like a methodical and premeditated act on his part, my tiny bare feet were covered with the thorns of those rose bushes!

How many were there? Twenty or thirty perhaps; at least that was how it seemed to my young mind. Yet the thorns in my feet were not nearly as painful as the confusion I felt over why someone would pretend love with the seeming intention of inflicting such a cruel experience.

My mother carried me inside the house to the bathroom and sat me on the side of the tub. As she extracted the thorns one by one, I clearly remember watching her face, deliberately searching for some definable expression, hoping for some utterance from her that would at least settle my confusion, if not the physical pain. To my dismay there was only silence. The only explanation I was afforded was simply what I was able to glean from her eyes as she glanced momentarily into mine between the tweezing of each thorn.

It seemed my mother was as confused as I was. And as I surrendered to the absence of the comfort I longed for, the pain of the thorns coming out of my feet was even greater than when they entered. So, I decided crying was an appropriate release, and if others believed I was crying only because of the pain in my feet then let them, because certainly no one else could actually feel my pain. Nor were they capable of undoing what had just happened to my heart, which hurt much more than my feet. And so, until now, I kept the true reason for my tears a secret known only to myself.

CHAPTER 2

A Child's Faith

"God writes spiritual mysteries upon our heart where they wait silently to be discovered." ~ Rumi

THEIR NAMES WERE MARY AND JACOB, an elderly German-Jewish couple who my family always referred to as Aunt Mamie and Uncle Gockey. They were actually friends, albeit, very good friends to my mother, and they sometimes watched my siblings and me on weekends and after school.

Gockey was a kind old man. He loved playing silly, harmless jokes on my two older brothers while he sat like a jester on a throne in his well-used, over-stuffed rocking chair situated in the dining room where he could watch Mamie cooking meals. Each time Mamie heard the noise of scuffling and laughter from Gockey and my brothers she would heartily scold Gockey in her accent, telling him "Stop it Yacob!" I was certain he did not take her very seriously, though. He would simply grin and chuckle, as if the sound of her demand was the joy of his heart, his eyes shimmering out from what looked to my young eyes to be a terribly wrinkled old face! My brothers and I had little doubt Gockey would soon sneak another joke on them. Of course, neither did Mamie doubt it.

It seemed the love between Mamie and Gockey connected

them by cords so strong they were quite nearly visible, at least to me. Then one night when I was six years old Gockey died in his sleep. I remember thinking, that is how I want to leave this place, peacefully in my sleep. A few weeks afterward, my brothers and sisters and I were visiting Mamie again. We nestled in the living room on the bed that had become the largest piece of furniture in the room since Mamie was no longer able to climb the stairs of her narrow, three-story home. A few of us were watching cartoons, while others were occupied with coloring books and crayons. I tried to be content with both activities, but found my attention continually drawn to a plaque hanging on the wall at the entrance of the staircase a short distance from the foot of the bed. It wasn't there the last time we were at her home, and although I could not yet read well enough to understand the entire message written on it, I could tell it spoke of peace, and heaven.

Finally, after several minutes of studying the plaque, I quietly left my place with the others sitting on the bed and climbed up on Mamie's lap where she sat in her own over-stuffed, well-used rocking chair in the same room. I felt unsure about how to pose my question, or if I should even ask it at all, but I would never be satisfied if I held it within me. So, I moved my cheek close to Mamie's cheek, and whispering, I asked her to tell me where the plaque came from. She whispered back as if I was the only one who should hear, telling me, "It was there when I woke up in the morning after Gockey passed away in the night." I did not say another word. I simply stared at that plaque wondering how the angel was able to get the nail in the wall without waking Mamie from her sleep.

Since then, I have realized the truth that every sincere question will be answered. "Seek and you shall find." And as if I have been led like that same child by my hand, it seems my journey thus far has been a gradual, deliberate unfolding, revealing miracle upon miracle, answer upon answer, and enlightenment upon enlightenment, illumining my own inner contemplation of what truly defines God's love toward us.

CHAPTER 3

Home Is Where the Heart Is

BY THE TIME MY OWN CHILD, Jesse David, was six years old, for more than a year we had attended countless doctor appointments. In fact, this had become a regular activity for us, and the attention he'd become the center of, coupled with the sense of urgency I felt, sent forth a clear message to him that the situation was in no way casual.

> *"My soul is from elsewhere, I'm sure of that, and I intend to end up there."* ~ Rumi

One afternoon as we were driving home after school let out for the day Jesse spoke up from where he sat in the back seat of the car with the kind of elation that we have all felt at times of enlightenment. His tone and enthusiasm were all about a great "Aha" moment for him that broke me out of my own consuming thoughts. I was thankful for anything that would draw me out of my burdened world of concerns, but as the message he so joyfully expressed flowed into my thinking mind, my own elated expectation immediately became confusion which quickly transformed into shock. Connecting the few words as he spoke, the same way we carefully draw a line from one point to the next on a connect-the-dots puzzle, the picture revealed

7

a foreshadowing of my worst fear. "I hope I die soon!", he said almost ecstatically. My first thought was that I didn't know how I would live without him. Then I began to wonder if his message was an indicator that he would not be with me for as long as I hoped he would be. I glanced at him for a quick moment and said in my dismay, "Jesse, why are you saying that?" And in that whirlwind discourse, he enlightened me to what seemed so natural to him, telling me, "Because I want to be with Jesus." I glanced again behind me only to see his face beaming, as if he had just uncovered the meaning of Life Itself, and I wondered if all of heaven was bending low to marvel in that split second. Had the entire Universe waited eons for this exact moment – his words and my awe? I was torn in my reactions and grasped for something to say in response, but the only words that came to me were, "Well, that seems like a good reason."

When I was the same age as Jesse, once again I was with my brothers and sisters at the home of Aunt Mamie. It was a warm, bright Saturday morning and we were outside in the front yard. My oldest brother, Johnny, drew our attention to the sunflowers growing on one side of the yard next to the fence. In the opposite direction I could see the highway from the hill Mamie's house stood on. My attention was drawn to that highway. I wanted to go home. I stared at the road and pictured every turn, left and right. All I had to do was give my brothers and sisters time to become involved in their activities enough that they did not notice me. Once I was invisible to them, I simply had to begin walking. And that is precisely what I did!

As I embarked on my journey, I remembered with each step I took the instructions my mother gave me to never get into a stranger's car. I walked quickly, approaching each turn and crosswalk with alert caution, hoping to remain unnoticed to passers-by, but alas, after only a few blocks my trek was halted when a car with two men stopped. The driver called out asking me where I was going. "Home!" I told them. Then, to my dismay, the one driving the car got out and approached me, determined to get me into that car! I struggled and fought to get away, but I was no match. So, there I was, in the back seat of a stranger's car, and yet as odd as it seemed to me at the time, I sensed no danger whatsoever. Nevertheless, I was extremely upset, not only because my journey had been so rudely interrupted, but more importantly, this unexpected and disturbing revision to my finely thought-out itinerary created a breach of my promise to obey my mother, and I did not want to lose her trust in me.

At first the two men weren't sure what they should do with me. Then they turned their attention to where I sat wondering "why all the commotion?" They asked me, "Where do you live little girl?" Well, that was simple enough I thought. "832 58th Avenue!" I told them, and I even directed them how to get there. They looked at each other for a moment as if I had spoken a foreign language. Then the driver said to the younger male passenger seated next to him, "Do you think that's right?" I interjected firmly, "Yes!" They were both quite puzzled and I couldn't understand why. It seemed so simple to me and yet these two men were delaying my arrival. As they drove in the direction of my house, I listened as they began discussing my father. As it turned out, they had known him for several years. They parked in front of my house and as the three of us walked to the front door I was quite uncertain what reaction I would get from my father and mother, but that didn't matter to me. I was home, and that was all I cared about.

Well, I still feel that way. I cannot wait to be home - where Jesse David is, but in the meantime, I am not willing to waste any of the time I have left here. It is important for me to live in gratitude, with dignity, recognizing that everything we are supplied with, whether it be money, relationships, knowledge, well-being, and even the time we are given, is from the Source of all creation, entrusted to us for our constructive use.

Shortly after Jesse transitioned, someone asked me what it

is exactly that drives me at the core. My answer was immediate and simple; "Love. Just love." In reality, this is true for all of us, and perhaps every so often this motivation will spark our feelings and imagination, but what would be considered the markers on an individual basis that characterize a consistent trend toward an expanding, permanently sustained out-picturing of this ultimate, original, divine purpose in one's life, and where do they originate?

I have often contemplated the story of Jesus at the tomb of Lazarus. I've wondered why Jesus lingered for days before making his way to the place where Lazarus was laid to rest. And why, as the account is told, did Jesus cry when He approached the scene? Is this evidence of Jesus' deeper connection to humanity even though we are taught he came to demonstrate His divinity? What was it that moved Jesus so deeply? He certainly must have understood the vast ramifications of reviving a human life from the grave. Pertaining to the body alone, resurrecting the man would mean more than simply waking a sleeping soul. It would require resuscitating every function at the finest and most critical atomic and cellular level throughout the entire physical structure even before Lazarus opened his eyes once more or took his first breath for a second time. Moreover, what of the agreements made between Lazarus and his Creator for his own life? Was it right for Jesus to intrude the demands of the mourners upon Lazarus? Would Jesus perform such an act simply because the people required it of Him? Or did Jesus draw Lazarus from the tomb as a preview of things to come? Would His own resurrection more likely be embraced if they witnessed first-hand what was to come?

Jesus' ministry was coming to a close. Time was running out and there were few indicators the people actually understood the reality and power, much less their own inherent authority and responsibility in the words Jesus spoke when He said, "I Am the resurrection and the life." (WEB, John, chapter 11, verse 25) Perhaps He cried because, not unlike many of us today, the followers of Jesus still did not realize that whenever He spoke the words "I Am" He was not only decreeing for His own life, He was actually teaching the precise means by which each of us must also raise every activity of life throughout the entire earthly realm into the greater perfection, beginning with our self and then extending it to all life, the structure of the earth, and even the atmosphere around the earth, until we, too, become the resurrection and the life.

This account is to me among the most impressionable acts recorded of Jesus, and I am stirred by Jesus' command of Lazarus to come out of the tomb. Can it be possible to send forth a command so powerful that even the non-beating heart, the ears that hear only silence, and the eyes that see only darkness awaken with a will to comply though still bound by the shrouds of Sheol? Assuming this account is accurate, I imagine the command sent forth by Jesus was intended by Him to permeate the densest of this physical realm, from the deepest darkness to the heights and extremes of heaven's infinite reach; a command drawn from the very source of Eternity and Life Itself, reverberating enough power to penetrate not only the tomb of Lazarus, but the soul of every individual who has ever embodied, or who ever will. Was this not a command to every life? Am I not Lazarus in some way or another?

I have come to believe that before we ever enter this world, we each make agreements with none other than our self with the intention of drawing into our life the perfection that will become our eternal attainment of our own mastery and victory over all matters. Every thought, word, and deed become an opportunity to raise the human - the ego, with all of its own intentions - into the greater perfection until at last we are released of human bonds and the eternal, self-sustaining protecting perfection is revealed as the Master Control over our use of the divine powers and gifts of Life ever expanding.

Throughout my journey, searching out the truth and purpose for my own existence, I have come to believe that one of the reasons we are here is to develop our eternal character by practicing the very things we will be doing for eternity. And if we are ever actually going to do the things Jesus did and greater, as *He* spoke, then we must begin to do the things He taught us while he walked among us, the very things He himself did. This is a marker, indeed, and a beginning.

CHAPTER 4

A Reason for Rainbows

Life, that Universal Energy acting and poured forth from the very Source of Life Itself, will always give more than we could ever return by our human efforts, but the mere recognition of this magnificent activity of Life is the beginning of enlightenment, mastery, and opulence ever-expanding and permanently sustained, and nothing, aside from our own choices, can ever hold it back. ~ PmCornett

WE WERE NEVER SURE WHAT TITLE to give Priscilla. She was simply Priscilla. We'd always had a caregiver, and Priscilla was the third since I was born. I was five years old when I first met her. My parents interviewed her for the position one evening and I recall watching her and listening to them speak to each other. Within only a few minutes I knew she was the one, and I was so thrilled to meet her that before she left, I wrapped my arms around her and tried to pick her up, though she and I both knew the effort would be greater than the effect. Nevertheless, I had to try, if for no other reason than to satisfy my own curiosity, and perhaps also make a mark on her memory strong enough to solidify and seal our friendship from that moment forward.

Priscilla came to our home Monday through Friday each

week for the next eighteen years without fail. She loved us as if we were her own children. In fact, when my mother was expecting my three youngest siblings, Priscilla always referred to having six, seven, or eight children, adding, "And I'm expecting another one."

I am the oldest born to my father, and although my mother brought my two older half-brothers into their marriage, my father waited through a succession of five girls before he was presented with the son he had always wanted. Finally, the day arrived. June 17, 1966. It was a hot, humid Maryland summer afternoon when my father and mother left for the hospital, and soon afterward a strong thunderstorm came through. Priscilla was cooking dinner for us, and I stood with a couple of my sisters at the large picture-window in the dining room watching the lightening and counting the seconds that equated to the distance the lightening was from us. Priscilla always had us wait to eat, or even stop eating, if it was storming at mealtime. She told us to "let God do His work", after which we could begin eating again. This time the storm passed before dinner was served, and as the rain let up and the sun peeked through dark, majestic clouds, we were amazed at the enormous, deeply colored rainbow that lay directly over our house. It was so brilliant and seemed so close I was certain that with very little effort I could actually reach out and touch it. When Priscilla saw the rainbow, she spoke up in all of her wisdom, which always amazed us, and said, "It's going to be a boy." We never questioned her wisdom. She knew these things. How she knew I could not figure out, but she was always right. A few days later our mother came home to us with our new brother.

Four more years passed, and just a few weeks before my thirteenth birthday, the afternoon of August 19, 1970 was a near replica of that day in June 1966. My father has taken my mother to the hospital one last time. Soon after they drove off, a thunderstorm came through, and just as before, in its passing, a brilliant rainbow lay directly over our house. This time we did not need Priscilla to tell us. We knew with a child's faith, and even announced to the neighbors, "Our mother is going to have a boy!" We did not doubt it for a moment. We had all the proof we needed - the rainbow. A few days later our mother came home with another boy child in her arms, and there was a peace about the situation. Certainly, I was at peace.

I have often reflected upon events such as these, and what they reveal to my heart is a beautiful out-picturing of no mere coincidence, convincing me I am not alone, and certainly I am not insignificant. Of course, my impressions are personal and subjective, but they have formed the foundation for the faith that has held my attention on that which is greater than me when I was being crushed, when I was being poured out, as it were, like water. And if it seems a small matter that after five daughters (for whom I know of no rainbows manifesting upon their entry into the world) my two younger brothers were announced so colorfully, there is more, much more.

CHAPTER 5

It Never Rains in California

I WAS FIFTEEN YEARS OLD WHEN, just around 8:30 on Saturday morning June 30, 1973, I heard my father's panicked voice calling for me to come help him. I quickly made my way to find him kneeling over my mother collapsed on the floor near the doorway of their bedroom. I watched him for several minutes trying to wake her. He picked her up and I followed behind him as he carried her to a nearby bedroom and laid her on the bed. He tried smelling salts and checked her pulse several times. One of my sisters called Priscilla who arrived at the house within the same hour. Priscilla and I tried to convince my father to call an ambulance, to get her to the emergency room, but he refused until nearly 12:00 noon. Within a few hours after she was admitted surgery was performed to drain a blood clot from her brain that was compared in size to a small grapefruit. The damage was permanent, leaving her paralyzed and comatose. She was only forty-one years old. About a week later my father took me to visit my mother in the hospital for the first time.

My initial reaction, seeing her shaven head accentuating her drawn face and the lifeless form bearing no resemblance of the beauty and poise I had always recognized as my mother was something I was not prepared for. I stood just inside the doorway of the hospital room speechless, in a state of dismay, unsure how to respond to the surroundings or the critical nature of my mother's state of being. I had never heard the words terminal or comatose – until now. No one told me I would see bandages covering holes the surgeon drilled in her skull to drain the clot that pushed her brain down onto her brainstems causing the massive irreversible damage.

I watched as my father quickly made his way ahead of me to the bed farthest from the door of her room. He called out to her, "Patricia? Patsy? I brought Patty here to see you." He signaled for me to come near, and I slowly approached to get a better view of this stranger my father seemed to know so well. I stared at her in disbelief, uncertain what to do, not knowing what to say, wondering what my role or responsibility toward any aspect of the circumstances should be, only to finally be rescued by a woman who with her very first step inside the room immediately took cool, calm control of the situation. She'd already met my father a few days before and was visiting her son in the next room who had been paralyzed in a car accident. Sensing my confusion, she put her arm around me and began to explain that my mother knew I was there and that she could hear and understand me, even if it seemed she was not aware. She taught me how to speak to my mother as if she could respond, demonstrating by speaking to her in a normal tone and expression. Then she encouraged me to do the same. "Say hello to her. Tell her what you want her to know. Most importantly, tell her you love her." It seemed quite strange to speak in such a manner to someone I was sure could not hear or comprehend, but I made myself do it. "Hi Mom. I love you very much." I did love my mother, and the circumstances were tragically overwhelming for me. But I practiced, no matter how awkward I felt doing so, and after a few weeks I was able to speak to her without any hesitation at all. And as her hair grew back, hiding the scars left from the surgery, I was able to recall her former beauty. Each time I came to see her I brushed her rich black hair, I wiped her face and arms with a cool clothe to refresh her, and massaged her hands and feet. I took up the role of helping to care for my six younger siblings as well as accompanying my father on visits to the hospital whenever he went.

After six months with no signs of improvement in her condition the hospital administrators explained to my father that the facility did not have the means to care for long-term patients. Arrangements were made to move my mother to a facility in Western Maryland. It was ninety miles from our home; still, I went with my father each Saturday, Sunday, and every holiday.

Over the course of the more than seven years that she survived that way there were only a few periods of intermittent consciousness that merely served to demonstrate the paralysis she suffered over the entire right side of her body and her inability to speak above a garbled whisper. After a while I learned to read her lips. "I hurt." she often told me. I knew what she meant. She was having muscle spasms that caused severe cramping in her legs and back. I always assured her that I would find someone who could bring her something to relax her, and then I would leave her bedside to scour the hallways for the first person I could find and implore them to bring my mother something to relieve her pain. At other times, she used all of her strength to tell my father and me "I want to go home." It was difficult to appease her pleas. At the time, my father and I believed she meant she wanted to go to the house where we lived. Now, I am not so certain she was referring to that. I have wondered if her pain wracked state and the isolation she endured day and night made her want to leave this world for her permanent Home.

There were many times, too, when the hospital called to tell us she was having problems such as pneumonia, or that she was experiencing some other type of distress, and we would make the unplanned trip to see her, often leaving within minutes of hearing the news. On more than one occasion the head nurse drew my father and me into a meeting room upon our arrival to explain that my mother did not have much longer to live, but she always pulled through somehow, that is until Labor Day, September 1, 1980. She was just forty-eight years old.

I helped my father make the necessary decisions and arrange the services for her, and three weeks later I made my own transition. I left the East for the West. Destination: Anaheim, California. I turned twenty-three years old the day I crossed the border into California with the man I had been in a relationship with for about four years. He had a wanderlust, and the promise of steady work with a property management establishment made it difficult for him to wait for me to be ready to make the move. Now, with only my concern for my younger siblings holding me back, I made what was the most painful decision of my life up to that point. I was deeply grieving my mother's passing which only added more dysfunction to the already struggling relationship my partner and I endured with each other. I never wanted to leave my brothers and sisters or the place I'd known as home all my life. In fact, over the years, when anyone asked me what brought me to California, I always said wild horses, and then I would laugh a little to cover up how strongly I really felt about it.

From the very first day we arrived in California, and for an entire year afterward, I struggled with such a deep depression that it became more and more difficult for me to function. Although I had decided to not begin working for several months, I took a part-time position at a fabric store located in a mall near where we lived. Sewing was a passion of mine and I was a fairly accomplished seamstress. I made most of my own office attire, and I'd even sewn entire wedding ensembles for bridal parties on a few occasions. My love for fabric seemed unquenchable, and I hoped that surrounding myself with what motivated me would help inspire me above the profound sorrow I was enduring. Every morning I arrived at the store before the doors opened for business and I set about various tasks such as re-stocking fabric bolts and vacuuming. Throughout the day I helped customers at the cutting counter, and I also learned the cash register. I was pleasant to everyone, and I don't think anyone realized my sorrow, until one morning a few weeks into my new routine.

It was a cool November morning and I left my apartment wearing a lightweight coat. When I arrived at the mall I parked near the back door of the store and made my way to the front entrance of the mall. I entered the store unnoticed and walked toward the back room to hang up my coat, but this particular morning was more difficult than any up to this point and I was uncertain how I would get through the day. Still cloaked in the coat I wore, as I approached the coatroom the door that exited to the parking lot came into perfect view. I realized my car was only a few feet from the other side of that door, and with barely a breath and no second thoughts, I just kept walking straight through that door. I got into my car and drove back home, all without a word to anyone or so much as a glance back. I knew I would not be alone when I arrived home. I also knew I would face a thousand questions about why I was not at work, and the only answer I could give was, "I can't do it." I just kept repeating the same answer, because I was so empty, so tired, and so depleted emotionally, I could not conjure up any other explanation. I was simply exhausted from the depression.

Within a few short moments the phone rang. The store manager was begging me to come back. She told me I was her best employee and she didn't how she would function without me there. I wanted to oblige her, but I simply did not have the strength physically or emotionally. After ending the call, I went into the bedroom and laid face down on the bed. I wanted to be alone, and I knew if given just a few minutes, I would simply stop breathing all together and there would be no more sorrow. I only needed a little time – alone. Instead, in an unusual turn of compassion, my partner came into the room. He asked me what he could do to help me. He laid next to me and he put his hand on my back. Oh, how I wished in that moment he had not done so, because that one, unfamiliar act of kindness was all it took to stop my release from the grief and sorrow consuming me, and I did not know how I would live day after day in such darkness.

A few weeks later, having given up the job in the fabric store, I decided to interview for other jobs. On one occasion I dressed in an outfit I'd sewn myself. I made certain my hair and make-up were presentable, and when I arrived at the small self-storage company located only a mile or so from where I lived, I introduced myself as the applicant scheduled to interview for the counter position. To my puzzled surprise, the woman who greeted me very politely told me, without proceeding with the interview, that she would prefer to "give the job to someone who really needed it." I never thought to tell her "that would be me". After graduating high school, prior to relocating to Southern California, I'd worked in positions with larger private-sector corporations. I seemed to land any job I sought, often right on the spot. This was likely the first time I had experienced such a rejection. I was clueless in those moments as to what made her say such a thing, so I simply thanked her for her time and realized I would not have been content there – at least not for very long.

By now the depression I endured was having an ill effect on every relationship in my life. I tried counseling on the recommendation of a relative of my partner who gave me the number of a renowned church just a couple miles from our home called The Crystal Cathedral. During the first session I was asked to complete a questionnaire designed to help the counselor assess my personality traits. At the second session I was informed that the results of the test revealed that I am "rebellious". Of course, I disagreed with that analysis, but that would be expected if I really am rebellious. Still, I pondered the label I was categorized into, and deep down I knew it was somewhat accurate. Aren't we all rebellious to some degree? My new status was never actually explained on a deeper level by the "counselor", but I thought certainly it would be addressed in upcoming sessions. That never happened, though. During the third (and final) session, a different counselor met with me. She seemed to have issues of her own, but I didn't turn down the opportunity to discuss the struggle I was trying to rise above. As the session progressed, I was astounded when the counselor became upset with my interpretation that God needed me in some way. She was disgusted at the thought, and held back no expression of disdain, telling me "God doesn't need you! What makes you so special that God would need you?!" I was stunned; neither did it offer me any new perspective from the one instilled in me from my earliest memories. I wasn't certain if I should feel ashamed or relieved by the revelation of God's very own disregard for me, but needless to say I did not go back there. I had enough of my own darkness, and did not need anyone else's heaped on me. And yet, no matter how I tried, I could not break free of the sorrow I was sinking ever deeper into, so after some discussion with my partner, in mid-November I arranged to take a train back to Maryland. The trip would take four days and I planned to stay with my grandmother on my mother's side.

I'd never been on a train before and only hoped the facilities would be adequate for freshening up each morning and getting some sleep at night. When the train finally embarked on the journey intended to take me back to the place that was familiar to me, I watched from the window next to my seat as we made our way through miles and miles of the most beautiful vistas I'd ever seen, passing through the foothills surrounding Los Angeles and traveling through the mountain regions of the entire Western United States. But the train moved so slowly through those areas I wondered how we would ever arrive within four days.

At 5:00 p.m. on the first day an announcement was made that dinner was being served in the meal cars, and after several minutes I decided I had better eat something to get me through the night. A train attendant escorted me to a table already occupied by a group of adults older than myself. Though I didn't protest, I was not comfortable with the arrangement initially. I wasn't good at pretense and I didn't want to have to hide the way I was feeling, but after some conversation and a small meal, I actually felt a little more light-hearted.

On day two at approximately 3:00 p.m. the train stopped in Chicago. This was an opportunity to step outside for a while and stretch out. The two days alone and the distance from the pressures weighing on me offered the freedom I needed to begin to catch my breath. I'd never been to Chicago, and though we didn't have enough time to sightsee, I looked around as far as I could see, taking in the view around the station and farther into the horizon to get a feel for the city and region. I entered the building a short distance from where the train stopped to use the public facilities, and on my way outside again, I noticed a directory with ticket prices for other destinations. I found the price of a return ticket to Los Angeles and realized I had just enough if I refunded the remainder of my trip to Maryland and added the little cash I had. It wouldn't leave me with any money for food, but I had taken some peanuts and other snacks I believed would surely hold me for the two-day trip back. Anyway, I wasn't certain I would be any happier back in Maryland. I only knew I was not happy in California. Perhaps I just needed to decide for myself where I wanted to be, instead of succumbing to the demands of what others wanted. So, I decided to give Southern California another chance.

I wandered outside and pondered the possible outcomes of each choice for a few minutes. I walked inside the building again and stood in front of the directory, staring at it as if it might actually speak something to let me know the right choice to make. A few minutes later I made my way to the ticket window of a kindly older gentleman who graciously refunded the remainder of my reservation and then handed me my new ticket and itinerary. I walked to the pay phone directly across from the ticketing booths and called California. When I arrived at the station in Los Angeles, I felt a sense of relief and gratitude. A few days later plans were in the making for me to host a Thanksgiving dinner in our home for the few family members who resided nearby. I felt good about it. Although I was never passionate about cooking, for a young woman I was a fairly good at it, thanks to the few secrets I'd gleaned from watching Priscilla. And I did enjoy setting a table for others to enjoy.

Within a few weeks I took a job with a small insurance brokerage firm where I handled all the front office duties. I was becoming better acquainted with my new surroundings, and as I lost my fear of the freeways that channeled what seemed like never-ending miles of bumper-to-bumper traffic and on-ramps that were nearly non-existent, I gradually gained a greater sense of independence. Letters arrived occasionally from my brothers and sisters back home, and that always helped me to feel more peaceful, too.

Precisely one year after my mother passed the relationship that took me to California ended, as did the severe depression I'd endured. I had my own apartment and was working a stable job, supporting myself comfortably, making new friends, and feeling stronger and more focused than I had ever experienced before. Once I realized I was going to be fine, I decided that even if it was only for having escaped the frigid winters of Maryland, I would be staying for a very long time.

A year later I met the man I would marry. Our ceremony was on January 12, 1984, and eleven months later I was pregnant. This was a true miracle since doctors told me several years before that I would never bear children. But around the tenth week there were obvious signs the pregnancy was not going to go full term. I had already begun to experience many of the physical changes of first trimester pregnancy when I learned the new life I carried was developing outside of the womb and it was necessary to surgically remove my left fallopian tube, thereby terminating the pregnancy. I was devastated. The doctor wanted to admit me for surgery immediately, but I needed time to let go emotionally. I needed to come to terms with all this experience would mean for me, as well as for the life I carried that never really had a chance. I told the doctor I would be in touch, and he admonished me to not wait too long because of the risk of the fallopian tube rupturing. I agreed and left with a heart as heavy as the earth itself, knowing I would do what was best based on my own timing. I needed time to pray, mourn, and just make sure the little life that trusted me in the first place would know I was sorry my body could not adequately provide a safe space to nurture it into the world.

I had it in my mind to give it two weeks and then arrange for the surgery, but about one week later I began to feel the most powerful contractions in my lower back that I could have imagined. I was surprised by how powerful they were, and I knew it was time to contact the doctor and schedule the procedure. I cried throughout the entire admissions process, disheartened and confused about my possible responsibility in the whole situation. I also knew if my fallopian tube burst, it would all be over, and that could possibly mean for me as well. In the years since, I have considered the possibility that because the pregnancy was outside of the womb, it may not have been developing normally. Then again, I will never know for certain, and so I rarely dwell on it these days.

Immediately following the surgery, in the throes of sudden termination, my body ached in ways no one prepared me for. Not only that, the outcome created an emotional cave in me, igniting a desire which until then had been mute, but now simply would not be quieted. And for the next five years I found myself at heaven's door, and I kept knocking on that door until one amazing day that changed everything about my life - eternally.

CHAPTER 6

The Science of Rainbows

I DON'T RECALL THE PRECISE TIME of year it was; January 1989, or there about. In the early evening hours, my husband was listening to a radio program while he reclined in the bedroom. It was being broadcast by one of the major non-denominational churches located in the Southern California area, and the discussion focused on open adoption.

I listened from the living room, reluctant to allow myself to succumb to any hope or enthusiasm. Neither did I not want to risk revealing just how deeply I was hurting, so I hid myself, hoping my husband would not realize my true reasons for not joining him for the program. I recalled the suggestion my obstetrician made during a follow-up after the surgery that my husband and I might want to consider adoption. At the time the idea of adoption did not sit well with me. I had the impression we would pick out a child from a facility or foster home and pretend it was our own. Such pretense would never serve to fill the void inside of me. But as I listened to the guest speaker on the radio program explain the process of open adoption my impressions changed. I realized that open adoption meant I would not only be a mother, but I would also be ministering to that child's birth mother in a relationship of trust. At the close of the program I decided to ask my husband if he would consider the option, though I knew we would have to be in complete agreement, so I told myself that if he said no, I would have to accept his answer and never bring it up again. Without hesitation his answer was yes, and soon afterward we began taking steps to learn more about the open adoption process.

We attended a one-day seminar held in March 1989. As we entered the expansive sanctuary of the ministry presented on the radio program, I felt intimidated, uncertain of the protocol for such an event. Within moments a receptionist welcomed our attendance and invited us to browse the various brochures, books, and pamphlets laid out on a table in the vestibule near the massive doors leading into the sanctuary. The material pertained to various aspects of the adoption process as well as other agencies that provide adoption services. We made our way into the arena-sized auditorium and found a seat two rows from the front of the podium which allowed me to see and hear the speaker without obstruction. Soon afterward the seminar began.

Initially there were only a few couples in attendance, and I recall thinking how that was a good thing, because I wanted to be assured our chances of being chosen were as good as sealed. All the while I tried to ignore the horribly frightening thought that my husband and I would be found simply not worthy of such a blessing, as if every imperfection I had ever created for my life, as well as those imposed upon me, would be blazed in front of the entire congregation of other hopeful adoptive couples.

The Founder of the adoption ministry opened the seminar. I listened closely and clung to every expression spoken from the podium as she and other speakers after her shared what was most important to them. It was impressed upon those in attendance that the child's welfare is always the number one consideration. Next in priority are the needs of the birth mother. The adoptive couple is always last in the arrangement, and I recall planting that crucial order of priority in my heart.

However, it may have been what was not spoken, the choices beyond the obvious ones, which transformed all the reasons I could ever think of for why I might be found unworthy of being chosen into being most worthy, chosen, and blessed. I felt so close, and yet still so far, from what I desired most - to be a mother.

LESSONS IN RETURN

As the seminar continued, I found it more difficult to contain the sorrow I felt for the bank of love trapped within my entire being. I could hardly breathe while holding back tears. I eventually lost track of how many couples were in attendance, and the activities that had taken place from the time we entered the building until almost halfway through the seminar took me from one extreme of hope and fear to the other. Aside from the various speakers, I was most aware of the husband and wife sitting in front of me. Then, one of the speakers mentioned the number of hopeful couples in attendance. I looked around to see what she was referring to, and to my severe chagrin I saw what appeared to be at least one hundred couples, each representing a chance we would not be chosen. Never had I felt so powerless! Never had I felt such jealousy, or competitiveness. And never had I felt so ashamed. I was ashamed I was even capable of feeling such things, all the while torn by a deepening despair over the growing void that seemed to be consuming me now.

I worked hard to conceal my sorrow, naively believing I was the only one in the entire group who had such a deep longing. And while I sat very still, listening, hoping, watching, and praying, to my astonishment I saw the hand of the wife who sat in front of us as she drew it gently toward her face. She touched her own cheek and wiped away her own tears. I was surprised, and at the same time relieved, as the tangled web of emotions I desperately worked to unravel began to dissolve within me. I was amazed to realize I was not the only one who hurt so deeply. Moreover, she had given me permission to let my own tears flow. It was such a kind permission, and a much-needed release. And though I never looked into her eyes, the momentary glimpse of the one small act she refused to withhold changed all of my fears into the very compassion I so desperately needed, and all of my self-desire into a longing for the healing of another's heart. I wondered if she hurt for the same reasons I did. Then I considered what I would do if I were given the authority to take for myself what I had longed for so deeply for so many years.

As I pondered this imaginary privilege, I knew there was only one truly loving choice that could be made; a choice which transcended every reservation and fear. I played the scene over and over in my mind until I was able to make my choice without any feeling of loss whatsoever. Again, and again I watched as I placed in the arms of the woman who sat in front of me the child I had waited to love for so long, because I believed if this woman was not afraid to show her tears then she would not be afraid to show her love. A love without fear is a love without limit, and that is how I must be prepared to love the gift, the heart and soul of the miracle I prayed for; the child I just wanted to love.

CHAPTER 7

Love with Arms Wide Open

AUGUST 1989 MY HUSBAND AND I met with a representative of the adoption ministry to present our resume containing a biographical history for each of us, professional photos, and a completed questionnaire. The entire resume took five months to complete. After a brief interview with a counselor our resume was placed on file, leaving nothing more for us to do except wait. During the weeks and months that followed I asked God in prayer to prepare me. I asked God to give me a child for only one reason; Love. I wanted to love a child, just that simple. Eventually, I became more specific, stating in detail the manner in which I desired my prayers to be answered. In time, I began to pray with a boldness mixed with humility, understanding that God remained the Director of the fulfillment of my prayers and the Creator of the life entrusted to my care, if my prayers would even be answered at all. Each time I came to God in prayer I felt more confident, making every detail of my desire known as I approached with my requests, until finally I told Him, "And by the way God, can my son be born in March?"

Five months passed from the time we placed our resume on file when we received a call from the adoption center explaining that a birth mother had chosen our file from the many resumes sent to her, and she would like to interview us. The caller told us the baby was due March 2ⁿᵈ, a mere six weeks away, and the doctors were certain she would deliver a girl. We spoke to the birth mother by phone for the first time on January 18, and made plans to meet in person during a visit at her home the following Saturday. Going forward my husband and I arranged to visit with her every other weekend until her due date.

As March approached, we anticipated with great excitement our new arrival. I purchased a few items of clothing for the baby and prepared a bassinet and other necessities. I was also given three baby showers; one with family, one with co-workers, and one with friends. Then, with only a few days remaining until the baby's due date, I packed a suitcase in preparation for the trip from Orange County to Visalia, California. The time seemed to pass more slowly even as the due date approached and then passed. Though I tried to relax, I often found myself counting the hours and minutes uninterrupted by the phone call we waited for, with the exception of a couple times when we received a call from the birth mother to assure us that the doctor was closely monitoring her and the baby, and they were both fine. Then, in the early morning hours of March 14ᵗʰ, we received a call telling us the baby's birth mother was on her way to the hospital. We loaded our suitcases into our car and set off for Visalia. The trip would take approximately four hours and since the birth mother told us we could witness the delivery if we wanted to, I was anxious to get to the hospital as quickly as possible.

We began our trek at approximately 5:00 a.m., and making our way through the early morning rush hour traffic along the freeways of Los Angeles just as the sun was beginning to rise, I mentioned the beauty of that scene. Perhaps that is what sparked my husband's memory, and he said enthusiastically, "Oh, I forgot to tell you. I saw a rainbow yesterday." He knew the story of the rainbows when my younger brothers were born, and I knew the reply he was expecting. I said, "Well, then it's going to be a boy." He just shook his head with a grin on his face, as if he had intended to get that very response from me whether he believed it or not. I, however, was certain my awesome, powerful God could answer my heart's prayer, and I did not mention it again.

Jesse was born at 7:50 a.m. We were greeted by the birth mother's brother when we arrived at the hospital around 9:30 a.m. He walked us to the nursery and standing at the window he pointed out the bassinet with the name Baby W, and he happily announced, "There's your son." In that moment I gazed upon the most beautiful sight my eyes ever beheld crying at the top of his lungs, perhaps in protest of the blue knit cap a nurse was putting on his head, so I cried too. Well he simply was not going to go through anything but that I would be right there with him, so crying seemed the appropriate thing to do.

We visited with Jesse's birth mother over the following two days. The time progressed quietly. A dedication was planned for Jesse David, after which we exchanged gifts as tokens of the relationship we would build throughout the years. Then, when it was time for Jesse's release, I had a sudden and overwhelming sense of the feeling of loss Jesse's birth mother would experience once we left her hospital room. I cried, feeling torn and humbled to think of walking away from her with the child she was entrusting to my care. Is there anything more sacred or more humbling than to be trusted with another human life? In the very same moment I knew the answer, and I felt it with all the gravity that could ever be realized.

A court-established wait time of six months allowed the birth mother time to reconsider her decision before the adoption process could be finalized. During those months I kept reminding myself that until the adoption was finalized through the courts, this child was not mine. Rather, he was trusted to my love and care, just as he would be loved and cared for by his birth mother. Certainly, I was waiting for that moment when I could freely let the bank of love that I felt for this child flow out to him, but until that moment arrived, I would be his Watch-Mother. And realizing my accountability to God for the handling of this precious life, my thoughts toward him continually were simply to love him as perfectly as I knew how to love a child, but with arms wide open.

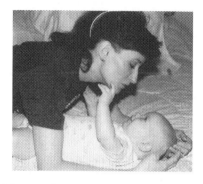

Mom and Jesse David (4 months old)

CHAPTER 8

The Visitor

"The meeting of two personalities is like the contact of two chemical substances: if there is any reaction, both are transformed."
~ Carl Jung, Modern Man in Search of a Soul

WHEN JESSE WAS ABOUT FOUR WEEKS old, we received a call from his birth mother. She told us she would be working in the area where we lived, so I encouraged her to visit us. It was late in the evening when she arrived accompanied by a friend and Jesse was sleeping soundly. I gently lifted Jesse from his cradle; he slept through the movement, his head resting on my shoulder. At her first glimpse of him, she was amazed at how much he had grown, and she spoke out, "My God! Look how big he is!" Then, to my utter amazement, Jesse David lifted his head and looked around the room with a groggy, slow-motion movement that was quite surreal. He knew the voice and he was going to find it. I laid him in her arms where she sat on the couch next to her friend, and it seemed both she and Jesse David were very peaceful. A couple weeks later we arranged to visit with Jesse's birth family. Jesse would be meeting his birth siblings for the first time. When they arrived, with just one glance they loved each other with a love that would not diminish as the years progressed.

The adoption was finalized in a ceremony at the courthouse in Santa Ana, California on November 13, 1990. During the first three years that followed we visited with Jesse's birth family on several occasions, sometimes in March to celebrate Jesse's birthday, and at other times during the summer months when we could enjoy the pool and outdoor activities. As time moved on, his birth mother became more comfortable with our relationship and the adoption choice she made. This comforted me for her sake. I loved this child as if a piece of my own heart had been taken from my body to form him.

Jesse was a happy baby. He was always smiling, and of course he loved to be held. He simply wanted to see everything, and never seemed to miss anything. His first word was "Daddy", and he took his first steps on the very day he turned eight months old. Around the same time, I was trying to teach him to wave hello and good-bye, but after several weeks he didn't seem to be catching on to the gesture. He never had any trouble picking up new mannerisms and learning new activities, so this was very puzzling to me, until one very enlightening day as I wrapped up a visit with a friend. Holding Jesse in my arms and saying good-bye to our guest at the door I decided this time I would not help him make the gesture. I wanted to see what he would do on his own without my interference. I began waving good-bye to our visitor, and within a few seconds, to my astonishment, Jesse David reached for my hand and placed it on his forearm. Then with his free hand, he pushed and pulled my arm in and out to make his own hand wave good-bye, simulating the same movement I had been using to teach him to wave. In that moment I knew I had a very advanced soul in my care for whom, in the final analysis, I would be held accountable for teaching and guiding.

In the Spring of 1991, we engaged the services of an au' pair agency to arrange a live-in who would help care for Jesse since I was working full-time. Regina came to us from Dresden, Germany. She had an excellent command of English, and her desire to perfect it gave her the incentive to teach Jesse. As a result, Jesse knew the entire alphabet and could hold full conversations by the time he was 18 months old. However, a year later Regina left to return to her home in Germany. I grieved to lose someone who had been so special in my life. Throughout the time she spent with us, caring not only for Jesse, but for me as well, she demonstrated trustworthiness unlike anyone I'd known. It was during this same time that my husband I divorced, although we were committed to raising and nurturing Jesse with the love that we always intended for him from the beginning.

Jesse loved conversation. He contemplated every aspect of life's mysteries, joys, and complexities. At three and a half years old, around 3:00 a.m. on a warm Southern California night when neither of us could sleep, I gathered Jesse up and held him in my arms while we talked about all sorts of things. The window in my bedroom was open, and I could hear a mockingbird calling out its various songs, so I said, "Jesse, Jesse. Listen. There's a bird singing in the middle of the night!" Jesse listened for a few seconds, and then explained, "You know, Mom, there *is* such a thing as a family of birds." Amazed by his loving response, I told him, "You know, Jesse David, you are *my* family." Shortly afterward we both slept soundly.

By four years old, Jesse was well aware of life as it pertained to his world of experience. In fact, he informed me on a particular occasion when I used the phrase 'the world at large', exclaiming, "I know how big the world is, Mom." And I, having vowed always to give him meaningful answers to his questions to the best of my ability, kept my promise to never regard his questions as trivial. However, I never imagined he would ponder the worm, until the day he asked, "Mom, do worms have chins?" I hesitated to answer for the same length of time it took me to send up an urgent request for an answer to this question that Jesse could accept as reasonable. "No, they don't." I replied. He, of course, wanted to know why, and I waited anxiously for the answer we both needed, but there was only silence in response to my call. Then it occurred to me, if I open my mouth poised to speak, perhaps the answer would begin to flow. And as I did so, one by one I listened as the words formed, "Because the worms would trip on them." This was a perfectly splendid answer, and one that delighted us both.

Jesse David, age 3

Jesse David often caused me to seek out the all-pervading Intelligence that placed us here, sustains our life, fills our longings, and reveals every detail in the answers to our questions so that we are able to move on to the next level of responsibility until at last we have fulfilled our own agreements to Life, mastering every condition by the Divine Love which cannot fail.

CHAPTER 9

The Puzzle

As Jesse progressed through his fourth birthday, I had already observed for several months a worrisome pattern in his development. Although he had been in pre-school for about two years, unlike other children his age his immune response did not seem to be growing stronger. Instead, he always seemed to be congested, and colds and flu took a severe toll on him. From about three and a half years old to well into his fourth year Jesse had been on countless courses of antibiotics for lower respiratory congestion. Then, during the month of August, at almost four and a half years old, Jesse was hospitalized in a state of dehydration. I had no idea until well after the experience that he could have died. The veins collapse under states of dehydration, and the life-saving intravenous fluids required to treat the condition cannot be administered. After three days in hospital we were able to go home. However, prior to being released the pediatrician had a special test run on Jesse, although she did not explain exactly what it would determine.

Hospital staff brought a machine into his room and positioned it bedside. His left forearm was wrapped in a stiff band connected to a meter that registered readings displayed on a monitor on the front of the machine. Jesse found the procedure very uncomfortable as the band generated electrical impulses designed to draw out sweat from his skin. The reading was 77. The doctor immediately told the technician to repeat the test. The reading was the same. The doctor then instructed me to have Jesse re-tested at a time when he was not sick or congested. I arranged to have the test performed two months later, in October 1994 at the same facility, and I watched the monitor register the same results, still unaware of what the results would determine.

A couple days later while at work I received a call from the pediatrician. She told me Jesse had a condition called Cystic Fibrosis. She went on to tell me it is a terminal condition, but that many patients were surviving an average life span of nineteen years. I was in a state of shock. I could not believe I was hearing the word terminal, and I could not accept that nineteen years would be the average age I had to look forward to with my Jesse David. My thoughts were spinning. My emotions completely derailed, I was unable to absorb any more of her explanation and told her I would call her back in a few days. I didn't have the emotional capacity to accept the news and needed time to come to terms with the unthinkable.

I recalled a conversation I'd had a few months prior with a co-worker whose child was the same age as Jesse. She was forlorn, wishing her child would never grow up. She wanted her baby to remain a baby. I told my friend that I could not wait to see the man Jesse would become. However, the news I'd just received made me wonder if that would ever happen.

Within a few days I contacted the pediatrician as I'd promised. She made some attempts to encourage me, but her words did not penetrate my shattered heart. Before ending the call, she referred me to a specialist at a nearby facility. I did not delay arranging an appointment, during which I was asked a battery of questions to help the doctor gain a comprehensive history of Jesse's symptoms. Based on the answers I gave to the barrage of questions he asked, and the check-up performed, this doctor believed that even if the diagnosis was correct,

Jesse would likely live a long life with few hospitalizations due to the relatively late diagnosis and general mildness of his symptoms. However, this specialist needed more diagnostic data to determine whether the diagnosis was in fact correct and he instructed me to have Jesse tested once more, this time at St. Joseph Hospital. He assured me this facility employed methods and protocols for such a test that are more specialized, and the accuracy of the results could be trusted with a very high level of confidence. I left the appointment clinging to the hope that further tests would prove the diagnosis to be incorrect, although that result would still beg the question of why Jesse was experiencing the symptoms that he had been expressing for more than a year by this time.

I observed Jesse closely over the next several weeks, afraid I would see any one or more of the several indicators I learned are symptomatic of CF. Over the short term of a month or so Jesse felt good and had no colds or flu. All the while I kept remembering the instructions that I still had not carried out to have further tests performed; tests that I hoped would rule out Cystic Fibrosis. Then, in January of 1995, I received a wake-up call, and I knew I had to stop denying the possibility of my worst fear and face my responsibility toward my child. Jesse began to complain of stomachaches after meals. Since he was not running a fever, I feared this symptom was due to the pancreatic insufficiency associated with CF.

I arranged to have Jesse tested again, according to the specialist's instructions. I watched as Jesse gave over both arms, each providing a much broader range of data to formulate the test results. The following day I contacted the facility to learn the outcome of the procedure. My call was placed on hold while the clinician retrieved Jesse's chart, and in the few quiet moments while I waited, noticing the music piped through the phone system, I realized the special day the rest of the world was celebrating. I prayed Jesse and I would have reason to celebrate, too. But the news I was given Valentine's Day, 1995, precisely one month before Jesse's fifth birthday, meant my hopes would not be realized. I listened, heartbroken, as the clinician read the results of the tests performed. "122", she said. I was crushed! This was a positive reading and much higher than the first three tests, although she explained the higher number did not necessarily indicate severity.

The specialist who reviewed Jesse's case a few weeks prior contacted me when the results came to him. He arranged an appointment for Jesse and me to meet with a team of doctors at a clinic near our home. This team of specialists focused on the management of a range of respiratory conditions, as well as those related to Cystic Fibrosis. And while we waited for the day of our appointment I concentrated on absorbing as much information as I could get my hands on and my mind around pertaining to Cystic Fibrosis.

On the day of our initial meeting with the clinic physicians I was prepared to discuss the most recent research, the direction and application such research was focused on, whether a cure was deemed possible in the near future, and the treatment protocols currently being applied. I understood the condition is genetic, and studies were ongoing in the field of gene therapy to correct the underlying disorder at Chromosome 7 which caused a malformation of the CFTR protein inside the cells that assists the channel that allows for certain nutrients to pass through the cell membrane. For more than five hours I drew out of these physicians all they had to offer of hope, probable prognosis based on Jesse's history, and the treatment protocol that would soon be implemented for Jesse's current symptoms.

At the close of the day the doctors told me no other initial appointment had been so exhaustive. They thanked me for coming to them having a solid foundation and understanding of the condition and the inherent implications that came with it.

STOPS AND STARTS

Life as we knew it would never be the same. Learning the new treatment regimens, as well as the protocols of the clinic, was overwhelming at first, but with practice we eventually became skilled in the customary methods prescribed for his diagnosis. I performed the chest therapy to release the characteristic highly viscous mucus from his lungs, he took the pancreatic enzyme capsules whenever he ate anything other than easily digestible fruit, and for the time being Jesse seemed to be thriving.

Then, at six years old and a year into his diagnosis, Jesse began to look quite pale and his stamina was extremely low. On a particular Saturday afternoon during a visit with my sister Gina and her daughter Carli, I watched Jesse while he and his cousin played together. I hurt for him, observing how weak, yet determined he was to find the strength to enjoy the mild-mannered games they played with the small figurines they manually put into motion using their child-imaginations while standing at the dining table. Gina brought with her some literature she'd gleaned from her own research on CF that gave details of studies on the positive effects of Selenium in the CF patient.

After Gina and Carli left, I made time to do my own research on the nutritional benefits of this mineral. I studied everything I could find on the topic; recommended doses, toxicity, what its purpose is in the normal, healthy body, as well as how and why studies reported it to have a positive effect in the CF patient. Once I had a good comfort level with the information, I started Jesse on a conservative dose of 50 micrograms daily. That amount equated to fifty percent of the recommended daily dosage for a child. To my utter surprise, within twenty-four hours his color was dramatically improved, and his energy levels returned to normal. I then added Vitamin C to his natural supplements. This regimen, along with the prescription multiple vitamin he took daily containing vitamins A, D, E, and K worked very well. For a period of about two years Jesse's weight maintained in a near average range for his age and height, and his lung function held in a positive state.

Jesse David, 4th Grade

Then, for reasons that were never explained to us, the clinic physicians decided Jesse should begin two inhaled medications. I watched and listened to the physicians confer as if we were not even present. It was as if they had no reason other than mere clinical protocol to begin the new regimen. Jesse was not experiencing noticeable degradation in lung function or exasperations due to bacterial colonization, and their decision created a profound level of distress for me. In fact, I tearfully expressed my concern to the RN involved in the decision before we left the appointment, explaining "Jesse is not a typical CF. His pathology is not following the patterns of the greater CF population. His lungs are virtually always clear since his nutritional needs were corrected." However, my words fell on deaf ears.

I was deeply distraught over this change. Nevertheless, Jesse and I incorporated the expanded regimen into our daily life; Tobi, an inhaled form of the antibiotic Tobramycin to control the bacteria in the CF lung, and D-Nase, also called Pulmozyme, used to break down the strands of DNA in the mucus that congests the lungs. I did everything to ensure Jesse faithfully complied with this expanded regimen, never realizing that over the next three years these medications, specifically the Pulmozyme, would eventually cause irreversible damage to his lungs and a cascade of secondary complications that would eventually change everything for his prognosis.

ONCE MORE FOR THE ROSES

In April 1999, I closed escrow on the purchase of a home in Anaheim Hills. The previous owners planted rose bushes along the fence, but they were not thriving, so I decided to try revitalizing them until I could landscape the yard thoroughly. However, given my early experience, those rose bushes intimidated me, so I decided to approach them in a manner of having made an agreement with them. I came to them in an attitude of friendship and as I approached, I silently introduced myself to them, rendering assurance that my intentions were pure. I remained humble as I worked around them, hoping perhaps they knew I was that same child who needed to reshape her early experience. Over time, I became more relaxed in their presence, little by little losing the fear I had learned so long ago.

"I will soothe you and heal you. I will bring you roses.
I too have been covered with thorns." ~ Rumi

While tending to the rose bushes I often meditated and pondered life and creation. And though I cannot remember my exact train of thought, on a particular day as I carefully clipped old blooms and pulled weeds from around the base of each one I began to realize that if the physical world really had been created by the spoken word, then there must be energy in the spoken word. Moreover, if the spoken word *is* energy, and if God is Love, then Love is not simply an emotion, it is actually Energy. This was an incomplete and somewhat hazy insight at best, but I pondered it from time to time over the next couple of years. I knew there had to be more; enough to make full sense of it, and I desired to draw forth the truth that seemed so tightly bound within it. I longed to grasp the beauty not yet revealed to my understanding, like the unfurled petals of the roses I tended. Even so, it seemed I had no more ability to draw forth such a thing before its time than I did to draw open a rose bud.

CHAPTER 10

An Answer

IN THE FALL OF 2001 JESSE began to exhibit more severe complications of the CF pathology. At eleven years old and the start of a new school year, Jesse developed a cough that became increasingly incessant until it persisted daily around the clock. It was a compulsive, dry, and unproductive cough, and at first, I considered whether he may have developed seasonal allergies, even though he never had allergies before. But after several weeks when the cough did not subside, nor did he seem congested, my search began for how to relieve this symptom. Sadly, it took me nearly two years to understand what was happening or to know how to help him. Neither did the doctors have a remedy. For nearly a year and a half Jesse struggled with this symptom several times every minute, literally twenty-four hours a day. I began to fear he would exhaust himself to the point of death. Jesse's lungs were in a constant state of bronchitis. Nothing I tried helped him, and I prayed continually for God to show me what to do. And that is precisely what He did on one amazing day in June 2003.

My sister Gina called me at my office. She was ecstatic, and frantically instructed me to "write down this word!" She spelled it out. "G-l-u-t-a-t-h-i-o-n-e". When I asked her to explain how she obtained the information, she told me she happened to stay home from work that day and by chance she caught a segment on the Today Show. A woman named Valerie Hudson, a Political Science professor and the mother of three CF children, was interviewed regarding her recently published research paper pertaining to Glutathione deficiency in the Cystic Fibrosis patient as a fundamental factor in the CF pathology. I had never heard such a long and strange sounding word, and it quite nearly made me want to stay away from anything to do with it. Still, I listened eagerly as Gina explained what she learned from the interview. Before we ended our call, she gave me Ms. Hudson's contact information provided during the show.

I emailed Ms. Hudson immediately. I had no idea what to expect or if she would even respond to my email, but within just a few short hours I received her reply which included a link to her research paper and a contact phone number. Her response was compassionate, and she expressed an eager willingness to collaborate and teach me all she knew. I told her I would study the paper, and she encouraged me to call her at any time if I needed to discuss questions about the research.

My gratitude was more than I could fully express. Hopeful that this was the relief Jesse needed, I contemplated how often during the two years leading up to this day I pleaded with God for an answer. I believed the information was somewhere and that God knew precisely what *I* needed to know in order to help Jesse. I had reached a point of exhaustion, overwhelmed and distraught for Jesse as well as myself, knowing at this point only what it meant to be poured out like water. Just days before, I made a commitment to God, telling Him if He would reveal to me the knowledge that I needed in order to help Jesse I promised to give credit to no other but Him.

I read Ms. Hudson's research paper several times over, diligently trying to absorb the many new scientific and medical terms, as well as the more complicated aspects of the CF pathology. I combed the material repeatedly, connecting the dots, putting the pieces of the puzzle together in such detail that it felt as though this new level of information was becoming a part of my physical structure. There was so much information the physicians never explained, and the scientific language was quite foreign to me, yet, I needed to grasp as much as possible so I could administer the supplement intelligently for Jesse. In the meantime, while I took several days to study the research, I purchased the highest dose of Glutathione available at a local health food store - 50 milligrams. And due to my lack of familiarity with the supplement, along with my uncertainty of the effect it would have on him, I started him on just 150 milligrams. Based on the research I was studying this amount was far less than the recommended dosage for Jesse's weight, but I believed it was better than doing nothing at all, while also causing no harm.

Less than ten minutes after Jesse took the Glutathione the coughing subsided - completely! Jesse and I were both astonished, and the relief that came over Jesse was nothing less than a gift of Life itself. I was thrilled and could not wait to share this news with Ms. Hudson. That evening, I placed an order with the manufacturer of the pharmaceutical grade of Glutathione used in the clinical trial accompanying Ms. Hudson's research.

As my understanding of the Glutathione supplement increased it became clearer what had been happening to Jesse's lungs in the years leading up to this. Due to complications of the CF pathology Jesse was experiencing a process of suffocation by toxic overload of metabolites such as peroxide, chlorine, and ammonia, produced by his very own body. In the absence of adequate levels of Glutathione, characteristic of the CF pathology, there is no way for the body to neutralize and eliminate toxic metabolites that naturally accumulate in the lung airspace. Jesse's lungs were on fire, in a manner of speaking. The poisonous accumulation had been deteriorating the normally phosphorus-rich protective lining of his lung tissue. Adding to this complication was the systemic imbalance of various enzymes and enzymatic processes caused by insufficient levels of extra-cellular Glutathione.

Making matters worse were the side effects of the inhaled pharmaceutical DNase, which I faithfully made certain he used as prescribed. After three years of that medication he'd become prone to lung bleeds. Since Jesse's lungs were not as congested as is typical of the mainstream CF population, there was nothing to protect his lung tissue from the DNase. This medication is meant to target the unbroken strands of DNA, deemed the culprit in the extreme viscosity exasperating the build-up of mucus in the CF lung. Instead, in the absence of the typical accumulation of neutrophils, the drug had nothing to act upon other than the very tissue of Jesse's lungs.

Mom and Jesse David, age 12.
Christmas, 2002, prior to Glutathione supplementation
and first in-hospitalization "tune-up".

I arranged an appointment with Jesse's pulmonologist to discuss our use of the Glutathione supplement and to ask them to track Jesse's progress. I was excited over the positive effects Jesse was experiencing and hopeful the doctors would also collaborate with me on this. Jesse had also been steadily losing weight over the course of the prior two years. As my concern over this increased, I began trying various methods to turn that around for him. I found various ways to add to his calorie intake at mealtimes, and mixed high calorie, high protein shakes for him which sometimes did not sit well on his stomach due to osmolality factors I did not understand at the time. All the while, it seemed odd to me that his physicians never mentioned his weight loss. Nor did they explain at any time leading up to this point the protocol for adjusting this aspect of Jesse's complications. On the day of our appointment I had high hopes and much enthusiasm. I believed the doctors would be supportive of my attempts for Jesse's increased wellness. Instead, I encountered a battle for which I was not prepared.

The physicians were severely upset with me. They admitted having been aware of the research on Glutathione deficiency in the CF patient for over four years, but because it was not FDA approved at the time, they took the stance that there was no evidence supplementation would be helpful. The doctor in charge of the clinic went on to demand Jesse be hospitalized that very day to have a G-tube placed for treatment of the weight loss, as well as be placed on IV antibiotics. I was stunned. I had never heard of these treatment courses before. The doctors never mentioned it, and even now they provided no explanation of what to expect from the treatment. I was not opposed to such treatment courses, if it were truly necessary. But given the invasive and sudden extreme nature of the demand, I asked for six weeks to observe Jesse's progress on the Glutathione supplement. I wanted to know if the Glutathione, along with the supplemental drinks I was making for him, would help him regain the weight he needed so badly.

Upon leaving the appointment I understood the pulmonologist strongly disagreed with my decision to add Glutathione to Jesse's natural regimen, perhaps because it would skew the results of their protocol, which I imagine their funding was based on, at least to some degree. I also realized he was very upset with my request to wait a few weeks to see if the Glutathione would have a positive effect on Jesse's ability to gain weight. So, Jesse and I made an agreement to do as much as possible to help him gain weight, and if we were not successful, or if he became sick at any time during the six weeks, then we would do as the pulmonologist directed.

A couple weeks later in August 2003, Jesse called me at my office. He was frightened and hysterical. I could not understand a word he was trying to say. I asked him to take a deep breath and tell me again what was wrong. He said two women from child protective services came to the door. I wrote down a phone number he read to me from the business card they gave to him and then quickly left the office. On my way home I called the phone number Jesse gave me. I was concerned about the impression they had of my ability to care for Jesse, and since they were there to investigate, I wanted to express to them not only the manner in which I was caring for Jesse, but every detail of my efforts for him.

The manager of the office of the Child Abuse Division of Social Services and a Registered Nurse returned to our home the same afternoon. I answered their questions, and they patiently listened for over two hours as I explained my research of the Glutathione study and my effort to help Jesse gain weight. As the discussion evolved, I realized this was an opportunity to draw to us an advocate, a force tragically missing from my life for Jesse David's sake.

When the meeting drew to a close this team of investigators expressed their amazement over our efforts and our love, and they agreed we were both fortunate to have each other. They continued to closely follow my management of Jesse's condition for the next two months. They made two more visits to our home during that time, and I took the opportunity to keep them as long as I possibly could, because I had no one else to express our life and efforts to who should care, or who did care.

It came as no surprise that none of these events added to Jesse's well-being. In fact, the stress took an even greater toll on his health, and in the midst of all this activity we also needed to prepare for the start of the new school year, which added to my concerns, because Jesse was still so weak. Then during the first week of September, just one week into the new school year, Jesse began to have flu symptoms. Neither had he gained any of the weight he lost over the prior two years. Instead, because of the stress of the circumstances, he lost more weight. Jesse and I knew it was now time for him to be admitted to the hospital for treatment.

Sunday afternoon I contacted the CF clinic to arrange for Jesse David's first in-patient admission to Children's Hospital. The on-call physician explained that it would be best to wait until the following day to admit Jesse when his primary physician would be available to devise the proper treatment course and follow him throughout their protocol. Sunday night we both tried to sleep as much as possible, though I still woke up to the alarms I set every three hours to administer the Glutathione supplement. Early Monday morning I contacted the RN from child welfare services to let her know our plan to enter the hospital. I was emotional and cried as I expressed my love for Jesse. She listened carefully and tried to be reassuring. Jesse and I arrived at the hospital mid-morning. As we went through the necessary steps to have him admitted I felt confused and frightened. I knew nothing of what to expect. The doctors did not explain the details of the treatment course or any aspect of what we would experience. I had no idea what would take place or what the expected outcomes would be, and I cried, fearing I was certainly losing Jesse. He was thirteen and a half years old, yet at just over five feet tall he weighed only sixty-nine pounds.

Once the Admissions Department finished taking all the information required, Jesse was assigned a private room. This was a comfort in itself to both of us. There was a great deal of protocol for us to learn, and at the time I did not realize that each CF patient is assigned a private room because their immune deficiencies and the bacteria they harbor require they be cared for under the protocols of infectious disease. This meant they must be isolated from other patients who may be carrying or susceptible to risks of infection that could further compromise their pathology. The level of activity was beyond our comprehension and exhausting by its nature.

Now, after so many struggles, he seemed relieved to be there. I felt it too; a kind of surrender in spite of the confusion and fear. He was taken to surgery for a PICC line to be placed on the inside of the bicep of his left arm just above his elbow. It would deliver intravenous medications into the blood flowing directly into his lung. Once back to his room and comfortable in his bed, in the midst of what seemed like utter chaos to me, the first of the treatment courses was started.

A liter-size bag was hung on the pole that also held the intravenous antibiotics. It contained a milky white fluid unlike anything I had ever seen. I asked the nurse what it was. "Intravenous Lipids" she said. I was amazed. The doctors never told us about this treatment, yet it would become the one for which I felt most grateful. At the end of the three-week treatment course, which I later came to know as a "tune-up", Jesse gained fifteen pounds. He also left with a G-tube we needed to learn to care for, feed, and change. We embraced this new regimen willingly, thankful now for any course that would offer hope for him. His ability to gain weight, along with our continued use of the Glutathione supplement, which the doctors came to accept, was our new strength and we felt a greater hope for the future.

Jesse David
Three-week in-hospital "tune-up" that included
IV nutrition and intravenous antibiotic.

Over the next two years Jesse thrived. He grew to over five feet eight inches and achieved 108 pounds. He looked beautiful and he felt good most of the time. And although he still experienced symptoms and went through a few more in-hospital tune-ups, we learned to manage most of these things with much more confidence.

During these years of strength Jesse enjoyed I came to know and understand him on a deeper and even more amazing level. We often discussed the hopes and dreams he had for his life, and I learned of his methods for managing activities among his peers at school, close friends, and even around me, so that his symptoms were less noticeable to others. The most profound awakening for me happened while the two of us were window shopping at the mall one afternoon. I remarked about his shoe – the same shoe – that always came untied. I had noticed it many times before and suggested ways he could tie it more securely. This time, while kneeling to tie the unbound lace, he explained that tying the string loosely allowed him a break to catch his breath each time he had to stop to tie it again when walking with his friends. To others he was simply stopping to tie his shoe, something everyone does, but for him, it was the private pause he needed in order to keep going without being noticed by others. As I listened, I marveled at his creative genius, and felt profound awe of him once more.

By the time Jesse entered tenth grade he had become accustomed to teaching the class lessons on any given day for his Math, English, and Science teachers. He understood the material, and it gave his teachers an opportunity to be both student and mentor. He chose German as a second language, and his confidence was at an all-time high. Students and teachers alike were drawn to his magnetic, insightful, and humorous personality. The only aspect of school we never seemed to resolve was Jesse's avoidance of homework, simply because it all came so easy for him. He comprehended the subject matter without needing to be taught, which meant homework was a waste of his time. He wanted to get to the next topic. Of course, since this habit was reflected in his grades, I saw it as a dilemma – until he finally told me that if he spent too much time on the small things, he might not have time to learn the really important things. That is how he put it, and again I was amazed by his wisdom for his life. Then one day, about mid-way through tenth grade, he came home with a book on Quantum Physics tucked under his arm that he'd borrowed from the school library. He was going to teach himself!

By this time Jesse had decided he wanted to become a herpetologist. He loved reptiles and observing the lizard's capacity to regrow its tail made him wonder if reptiles held a secret to curing diseases, especially those that effect the organs. He believed that if other species could regrow or rejuvenate parts of their physical form, then by understanding those mechanisms, it could be beneficial for human conditions as well, such as his own eventual need for a new liver.

Jesse also loved pondering the idea of perpetual energy, which he was sure he could find a way to produce, with one important caveat, he explained: "There really is no such thing as perpetual energy, because a catalyst is always necessary in order to start any motion." Still, we often discussed the idea, and the possibility that his discoveries, which he decided to call either "EE" for Exponential Energy, or "E^{2}", or simply "E Squared", might even win a Nobel Prize one day.

Jesse David's Reptile Birthday Party

Jesse David, age 13
Six months after starting Glutathione supplement
and Three months after "tune-up".

CHAPTER 11

I Became a Scientist – of Sorts

I HAD BECOME ONE OF THE more active members on the CF forum managed by Ms. Hudson from the time I learned of the Glutathione research in June of 2003. The forum supported the intelligent disseminating of the protocol for supplementing Glutathione, as described in her published paper on the topic. Discussions on the forum instantly sparked my enthusiasm to learn as much as possible about the underlying cause and pathology of CF, as well as the alternative treatments others were finding helpful. At the time I had little experience using the internet and at first, I didn't even know what a search string was or how it worked. Soon, though, I was able to navigate more efficiently and within a few weeks I embraced the World Wide Web as an invaluable source for the knowledge I was seeking. Terms such as "neutrophils", "ions", and "denitrifying" were no longer foreign to my vocabulary, and my skill increased in searching out the most important sections of published studies, all of which gave me greater ability to quickly pinpoint and gather information that might in some way help not only Jesse David, but the entire CF population.

I also began studying naturopathy, homeopathy, and aromatherapy. All of these methods utilize energy - the activity of various inherent rates of frequencies – to some degree or another. As I learned the mechanisms by which these therapies are effective, I used my knowledge of energy, along with other natural means, as a regular part of Jesse's alternative regimen. I sought out and incorporated into our routine regular checkups with a Naturopathic Doctor who was also an allopathic MD. Under his guidance I began giving Jesse a sublingual form of phosphorus to help rebuild the lining of his lung tissue, which not only helped reduce congestion, but also made him less prone to lung bleeds. Little by little, and with very close observation on my part, Jesse was able to go for longer periods of time without using the DNase or becoming congested, and eventually the CF pulmonologist agreed that Jesse could stop using the DNase. However, the damage done by that medication could not be reversed. He was still prone to lung bleeds, which we further managed quite successfully with supplements of the amino acid L-Lysine.

As other forum members realized my aptitude for understanding the intricacies of the CF pathology, as well as for researching alternative remedies, many of the members who needed the information in lay terms began to rely on my growing knowledge. I often helped patients and caregivers adjust their vitamin and mineral supplements, as well as the extracts and dietary support they incorporated into their regimens.

After only a few short months I received a personal email message from a forum member which included one comment that read like a sigh without any hope of relief. Yet, as I read her words, "I wish I could figure out how to eradicate the bacteria in my daughter's lungs", the simplicity of it all struck me. I wondered why no one had accomplished this already, and even though I did not have the slightest clue where to begin, I found myself propelled into a two-year investigation which, when complete, resulted in a hypothesis paper. In fact, I knew only two things; the names of the bacteria: Pseudomonas Aeruginosa and Staphylococcus Aerus. That certainly wasn't much to upstart my research, but it was worth trying. I typed two words in the search string: *Eradicate Pseudomonas*. To my surprise several results were returned, the most impressive being a study and clinical trial on the effects of the amino acid L-Arginine.

I learned that L-Arginine is a substrate for the production of Nitric Oxide in the body, and there was evidence suggesting that CF patients are chronically deficient in both L-Arginine and Nitric Oxide. I also learned that Pseudomonas is a denitrifying pathogen, consuming nitric oxide in the lung airspace, so it began to make sense that if the CF lung harbored these bacteria, then the environment of the CF lung must be such that the bacteria are able to thrive. Based on my research I believed that instigating the production of Nitric Oxide in the lung air space of these patients would reverse the condition of the environment in the CF lung that promotes an affinity for pathogens such as Pseudomonas to adhere in the first place.

I began posting bits and pieces of various related insights on the CF forum, but received very little feedback from the other members in response to the information I shared, with the exception of one young CF patient living in Somerset West, South Africa. He believed the information I was sharing was "a gold mine" as he put it. We kept in regular contact by personal email to discuss his vitamin supplements and other means by which he managed his care while I continued working for two more years to complete the hypothesis paper describing the many positive effects of GSNO (S-nitrosoglutatione), the product of Glutathione and Nitric Oxide when they are bound, on the CF lung. The paper also included a detailed protocol for mixing and administering the supplement for inhalation, as well as an oral regimen that would also provide benefits to the intestines and muscle tissue of the CF patient. I consulted with Ms. Hudson on occasion to ensure I was not over-looking key points, and when the paper was completed the young man residing in South Africa volunteered to be the first to use the regimen.

I contacted a distributor of raw chemicals and spoke with a sales representative. I explained that I was studying to obtain a Doctor of Naturopathy degree and described the research I was doing to provide a treatment for the CF population. He was moved and impressed with my efforts. Within a week I received the L-Arginine products necessary to make the buffered form of the solution suitable for inhalation. The shipment was inspected to ensure the product received was correct. Then the items were repackaged and sent on their way to South Africa.

I also searched out the contact information of Dr. Solomons, one of the researchers involved in the clinical trial of L-Arginine for inhalation in 1971, although I was uncertain that he would be willing to acknowledge my own work. After all, I was a mother and an IT professional, not a clinical or scientific researcher. And one more thing I could not claim to be was bold or intrusive. But after weighing the possibility of a rejection against the importance of the answers I needed to certain questions that weren't fully addressed in the research I'd done, I decided to step outside of my introverted comfort zone and make the call.

After silently rehearsing my introduction and the reason for my call several times, I nervously dialed the phone number in Colorado from my office phone. I was prepared to hear a recording asking the caller to leave a message with the promise of a return call within a given period of time that would never actually be received.

Instead, a woman's voice softly greeted me. My first thought was that I was speaking with an administrative assistant to Dr. Solomons, and I hoped she would be willing to put me through to him. After I introduced myself, I asked with whom I was speaking. She said she was the wife of Dr. Solomons. I told her the reason for my call, describing my research and hypothesis, much of which was based on the work her husband had done well over 30 years earlier. She explained that Dr. Solomons was not well enough to take my call, stating "he isn't able to speak", but she assured me that if I would share with her my questions, she would relay the same to him directly and return my call with his answers. I was deeply grateful for her response, and expressed my profound appreciation, as well as my wishes for her husband's full recovery.

When I hung up the phone, I knew there was a possibility that, depending on the gravity of his condition, I would not hear back from her. And even if I did receive the phone call she promised, was he coherent enough to give accurate answers? I could only wait and hope for the best outcome.

A few days later I received the promised response from Mrs. Solomons. She had accurately conveyed the two or three questions I posed, and the answers were precise and to the point. I was thankful for this, of course. Dr. Solomons gave me the assurance I was looking for regarding adjustments I'd calculated for measuring the quantity of each form of the L-Arginine to supply an individual three doses over the course of a single day. To do this, I simply computed the reduced measurements of the two forms of L-Arginine, as well as the amount of sterile water required, based on the protocol Dr. Solomons described in the clinical trial he conducted in 1971. His protocol required much larger amounts of the ingredients in order to supply the multiple doses of the treatment to each of the numerous patients involved in his study. He answered other questions, too, regarding possible toxicity, of which he confirmed there was no known toxicity associated with the use of the L-Arginine. He also strongly advised making a fresh batch of the solution every 24 hours, and to be certain to refrigerate the supply.

CHAPTER 12

Time in A Bottle

No time was wasted once I received the two forms of L-Arginine from the distributor. After ensuring the product was exactly what I ordered, I immediately repackaged the contents, and with the help of the mail clerk at my workplace, the items were en route to their international destination in Somerset West, South Africa. I tracked the shipment closely, and while it was in transit the recipient, who I will refer to as DJ, set about to purchase a scale that would accurately measure the miniscule amounts of each form of the fine white powder. He also purchased a supply of the sterile water required for mixing the solution from a pharmacy, and a glass container for storing the liquid. One week passed before he received the L-Arginine products. When at last he was in possession of the package we stayed in close contact to ensure he followed the instructions for preparation precisely as the protocol was written in my hypothesis paper.

On day one he used the regimen three times, taking the treatment every four hours, which called for a single nebulized dose of the inhaled form of Glutathione, immediately followed by a single nebulized dose of the L-Arginine for Inhalation, each measured at 4cc. The following day I received the much-anticipated email response from him describing the effects of the treatment. His precise and unforgettable words stated, "This stuff feels like silk on my lungs, and if this is what normal lungs feel like, then what does anyone have to complain about!" This young man, whom I've always referred to as my "Cup Bearer", enthusiastically described experiencing amazing improvements in lung function, including increased airway capacity and a higher concentration of blood oxygen levels, all of which worked to boost his stamina and general well-being.

When others on the CF forum learned of the results achieved by this treatment, several patients and parents of CF children also integrated the treatment into their alternative regimen. I would purchase the ingredients from the distributor myself to preserve the rapport and the availability of the product, and I often did not ask for reimbursement from the recipients, because many of the patients were living on minimal incomes. In return, I asked only that they communicate to me their experience with the treatment regimen, which were consistently very positive. Over the following three years I worked with several patients throughout the United States, including Florida, Texas, Pennsylvania, Michigan, and California, as well as patients living in Canada, Cayman Islands, and the Netherlands.

Jesse also used the regimen, and while I was certainly curious to know the results of his subsequent lung culture, I was not expecting the surprising results that showed no discernible trace of either P.A. or S.A., the very bacteria I was hoping could be eradicated by the regimen. His previous lung cultures always showed the presence of these two pathogens to lesser or greater degrees. However, soon after these events Jesse took his final downturn which was so immediate and severe that I turned my attention away from anything that was not life sustaining on his behalf. I felt certain I would not have time to submit the paper for peer review by a medical publication, so I offered the work to Ms. Hudson with my permission for her to post it on her website under the Utah Valley Institute of Cystic Fibrosis. **

** uvicf.org/researchnewsite/glutathionenewsite/GSNO.html

Within a few weeks clinical researchers recognized the work and contacted Ms. Hudson with questions regarding the results achieved by the regimen. She in turn forwarded their emails to me. I was more than happy to share the information with anyone who had the ability to take it into further study. It did not matter to me if I received recognition, the important thing was getting the information into the right hands. Within less than a year a clinical trial addressing the efficacy of the inhaled L-Arginine solution on the CF patient's lung was under way at The Hospital for Sick Children in Toronto, Canada. I was thankful for this, although I knew it would mean very little for Jesse David at this point. In September 2013 results of ongoing trials were published under the title "A randomized controlled trial of inhaled L-Arginine in patients with cystic fibrosis." *** Among the many conclusions detailed in the publication, it states that of the relatively small number of patients studied, Pseudomonas Aeruginosa was eradicated in two of the patients after two weeks of use. And a more recent study is currently in Phase II to determine the efficacy of inhaled Nitric Oxide in CF patients who have tested positive for P.A. ****

WHERE ON EARTH AM I?

November 2005, I had an experience that I can only describe as completely unexpected and thoroughly euphoric. I was fully conscious when, without any feeling of transition whatsoever, quite spontaneously and without any intention or effort on my part at all, I entered into a heightened awareness of a level of activity that seems to exist somewhere in the higher realms; a place perhaps where heaven and earth commingle, for lack of a

---

*** https://doi.org/10.1016/j.jcf.2012.12.008
**** https://www.cff.org/Trials/Finder/details/377/Phase-2-study-of-inhaled-nitric-oxide-in-people-with-CF

better description. I was here, but I was also there, in the midst of a peace that surpassed my understanding, experiencing a freedom that defied all boundaries and limitations as naturally as if I had always been there. The access to all I needed and capacity of mind - and body - to contain it were more expansive than I ever imagined possible. I clearly recall thinking that I first wanted to know all the information I could absorb about how to help Jesse. I remember knowing within my entire being that it was actually all so simple. I stretched out my arms, and as I did, I knew that simple motion was all it would take to draw into my consciousness the vast intelligence I required. I needed the answers to the questions I so desperately searched for; at least a hint or a clue to point me in the right direction.

When the experience passed, just as unprovoked as it had begun, I realized it was not enough time, and I immediately wanted to "go back". Feeling a sense of desperation to accomplish my task, and a desire to experience the peace and tranquility of that realm once again, I privately tried repeatedly to recreate a setting that was similar to when I was propelled there the first time, but nothing I tried caused the event to recur. After a few days I believed I was spending too much time trying to replicate the experience, and that I should instead set my attention upon combing over the details in my memory in order to preserve the experience and to draw out some truth that would become an anchor to hold on to when needed. I have thus concluded the lesson in the experience was to teach me a greater level of discernment of my own motives toward others, a lesson I have not forgotten.

Since that time I have recognized how often and how easily we rush forward to carry out our plans without examining the rightness of our motives toward others we may involve, and without ever taking a moment to realize there may be a reason beyond our own intentions for why we have crossed paths with another sacred soul. It is important to wait, watch, and listen, and if we are patient, we may find the purpose will unfold naturally. I have wondered, in retrospect, just how many of my own experiences were not what they seemed on the surface but were actually conditions acting as a substrate for a more profound eternal activity. I have observed that most everyone has a need to control something or someone, and individuals often become frustrated when others disappoint our unspoken expectations of them. We seldom realize the very first lesson in the use of the Power of Control is to first become our own Master in Self-Control.

As it turned out, the event I experienced and the insights I gained from it would become the very understanding I needed, an anchor to sustain me emotionally and spiritually, as Jesse David and I navigated the sacred and untouchable events destined to unfold only eleven months later, in early October, 2006.

CHAPTER 13

The Turning

I REALIZED WHEN I FIRST RECEIVED the news of Jesse's diagnosis there may come a time when, in retrospect, I would think of things I could have done differently for him, and it has been so. And always, whenever such thoughts come to mind, I find myself wishing I had realized then what I realize now, while at the same time also working to forgive myself.

It is so easy to become entangled emotionally over circumstances that cannot be changed, but I have learned to come back to the present moment by remembering I am still on my own journey. I have been given time to experience more of this world, time to notice the beauty and recognize the gifts that Life shows us in order to draw our attention to the magnificent Love that cannot fail. When I look at the moon and the stars set so deeply within a clear night sky, and when I see the glistening white snow that blankets the earth and trees during the cold Maryland winters, I instantly know once more that I am not alone, and peace comes to rest my heart and mind as I absorb such scenes from this earthly vantage point while I am still here.

With these thoughts in mind, I continue.

Christmas Eve 2005, on my way home from the office I picked up a large portrait of Jesse taken a few weeks before. It was hung majestically above the fireplace. And though there are

71

no words written on it, I have always thought of it as my plaque, like the one the angels brought to Mamie.

It was on this same evening, just one month after Jesse achieved his greatest level of well-being, reflected in that portrait, that he began to have severe nausea. For the first few days I believed he had the flu, but when a week passed and the symptoms were still just as severe, I contacted the clinic. The details of this episode became convoluted and difficult to sort through, even at the time. Nevertheless, after six weeks of trying to put the pieces of this new puzzle together, I finally realized these new symptoms began at the same time the GI clinic ordered a change to the supplement he took through the g-tube. I searched the label on one of the cans and read the statement "High Nitrogen Formula." This was something I deemed devastating for Jesse because he fell into a mere five percent of the CF population whose pathology includes an added gene mutation that causes rapidly progressive fibrosis of the liver. I speculated the high nitrogen content in the formula caused vasodilation – a dilation of the blood vessels, but due to the fibrosis, the blood could not pass through his liver. After only a couple weeks his spleen doubled in size, when it was already the size of a football, distending his rib cage and protruding his waste-line. Now his spleen also extended across his pelvic region and the pressure caused him pain throughout his groin and lower abdomen. I also speculated that toxins were likely accumulating in his system if blood pooling in the spleen could not easily flow through the fibrosed liver. I wondered if a toxic over-load may have been causing the nausea and endless vomiting that, no matter what I tried, would not subside, and in fact, increased as the days and months progressed. And to make matters worse, he dropped twenty pounds. Yet, no matter how much I pleaded, for some unknown reason the doctors would not agree to admit him.

Finally, in February 2006, the team of pulmonologists at the CF clinic took notice and arranged for Jesse's admission to the hospital. During the weeks leading up to his admission I had taken it upon myself to stop giving him the high nitrogen formula g-tube supplement supplied by the GI clinic pharmacy and instead made my own formula which fortunately Jesse was able to keep on his stomach. I used whole milk and added a protein powder supplement along with a pinch of Glutamine which is helpful in supporting major organs under stress. I blended and sifted the mixture thoroughly so it would flow through the g-tube without obstructing the device or tubing. I made the doctors aware of this, and though they did not want us to rely on the remedy long-term, we all agreed it was better that Jesse get the nutrition this provided rather than nothing at all.

Unfortunately, too much time had passed, and the downturn Jesse experienced during the weeks these events unfolded took such a toll on him that in my heart I believed Jesse's life had been cut even shorter. This time, upon admission to the hospital, the attending GI physician was someone we had never met before. However, I was determined he should not forget us. I expressed all of my disdain and frustration over the management of Jesse's care by the GI team for the blanket-change made for the G-tube supplement without any consideration for the individual patient's pathology. In fact, when I told the GI team Jesse's symptoms began at the same time his G-tube supplement was changed, they thanked me for my insight and admitted, "There may be other patients experiencing the same symptoms." I also expressed my heartbreak over the things Jesse was going through. Once it was clear this physician heard and acknowledged all I had to say and that more complaining on my part would not serve Jesse or the situation, I knew it was time to focus on the proposed regimen that I'd hoped would correct the problem and reverse the damage done.

From my perspective it seemed I was always doing damage control, most often because this facility focused on the general CF population. They pushed the same protocol on every patient, no matter their individual pathology. I knew Jesse was not a typical

CF, and clearly the protocol we were forced to incorporate was doing more damage than good for him.

Upon being discharged at the end of the three-week treatment course, it was obvious Jesse did not respond as he had in the past to the routine "tune-up" which included the intravenous lipids he received during prior in-hospital treatment courses. Not only was Jesse still severely underweight, the nausea returned after his CF doctor required that I stop the homemade supplement and begin using a different pharmacy-provided product. I always followed the instructions of the doctors, and in hindsight, that is one time I wish I had not! I could have simply received the delivered product and then tossed it out, as long as he was able to take the homemade mixture without vomiting. I also did not realize at the time that we could have simply opened the valve on his G-tube to release the substance accumulating in his stomach to relieve the nausea. However, I was not thinking as clearly as I did in the early years of our journey. Now, more than at any other time, I was giving in to exhaustion from worry, struggle, and lack of sleep. For Jesse, the nausea and vomiting persisted day and night, and I watched, feeling overwhelmed by my own inability to help him, while he was less and less able to eat or keep anything at all on his stomach.

CHAPTER 14

Returns on Investment

ONE YEAR PRIOR TO THESE EVENTS the company I worked for announced a merger and re-org with the promise of eventual layoffs.

In March 2006, after work one evening, I went outside to the patio next to the kitchen to wind down before approaching the activities of the evening. The remodel of the Anaheim house was complete, which included every room to varying degrees. Even the outside of the house was updated, and I felt a strong sense of accomplishment as I looked around at the changes. I had just settled into one of the patio chairs and started to relax when once again I experienced an interaction with the finer realms. I was enveloped in what felt like a soft cushion. It wrapped around my upper body and shoulders, and a very gentle nudge pushed me so that my entire torso visibly leaned forward. At the same time, a message vibrated through me which clearly translated that it was time to market the house for sale.

During the same week I also had a dream that the timeline for lay-offs at work had been escalated, and my release date would occur thirteen days sooner than my co-workers. The following week my manager told me that lay-offs were going to be implemented sooner than originally planned, and I would be among the first let go, since the system I alone supported 24/7 was running so smoothly that it required virtually no manual support. When I did the math, it turned out that the escalated lay-off schedule was thirteen weeks sooner than originally slated. Additionally, I later learned I was the only employee laid off in that round, which was set for the following week.

Early Monday morning I was set to meet with the personnel team handling my release. We went into a conference room where the details of the release agreement were explained, and although I was hardly enthused about the situation, throughout the discussion this team seemed conscientious enough. I'd been laid off a number of times in the six years leading up to this, always for the same reason, and the methods were typically cold and detached. I knew the routine all too well. However, this time I sensed an element of compassion on their part. In fact, I was surprised when near the close of the discussion this team asked me if I was okay with the termination date and severance package provided. I'd never been asked if I was "okay with that" at other companies when lay-offs occurred. "Yes." I replied. And yet, what choice did I have? Was any of this even negotiable? A thousand thoughts flooded my mind, many having to do with the way I was being prepared for the changes unfolding. It seemed that nothing I was facing was negotiable, and I didn't have the guts to risk not going along with a plan that seemed to be out of my hands, and yet perfectly orchestrated. The severance package provided my full salary for the following three months. Simultaneously, I was eligible to draw the maximum unemployment benefit that California provided for an extended length of time as long as I remained a resident of California. I was grateful. With my decision to sell the house, not only was I fortunate to have the financial means to take an extended hiatus from working, these provisions also meant that I could be with Jesse one hundred percent of the time, completely wrapping my life around him twenty-four hours a day.

The timing of these events could not have been better. Jesse and I loved going everywhere together, and among the most enjoyable aspects of the time we spent was the way we talked about everything. He loved conversation and he was quite accomplished at the art of it. Sometimes he would even find me while I fixed my hair and make-up before leaving to run errands together, and we would talk about whatever was on his mind at that moment. Sometimes we discussed his friends. He loved each of them as a friend for life. Other times, we devised plans for our life. Perhaps most often, we talked about ways to help him thrive. However, by this time the months of persistent nausea and pain had become too much for him to bear. Neither were my attempts to stabilize him successful. Having endured these symptoms for five months, in April 2006 he began to insist we seek out liver transplant options, so I contacted his pulmonologist

In the meantime, I also searched out a real estate agent to list the Anaheim house. It took three tries before finding an agent who knew how to market the house properly. Carrie was amazing. She helped in many ways to stage the home beyond what I was able to do in the limited amount of time we designated for getting the home listed. She had landscapers groom the back yard, and they retouched the front yard which was regularly maintained and already fairly presentable. She arranged a photographer to take several photos of the home for inclusion in a premier listing publication. I purchased this house in March of 1999 for $229,000 and now, seven years later, most of which was spent remodeling room-by-room, the booming real estate market meant this home would bring a sizeable return on my investment. Carrie and I discussed the most recent comparable sales in the area and agreed to list this home at $649,000; nearly triple the purchase price when I bought the house. I signed the contract after meeting with her one last time in our home, and on her way out she placed a boutique style for-sale sign in a strategic area of the front yard before returning to her office to add the listing to the MLS.

A couple hours later I happened to see from the front entry

window a vehicle stopped in front of the house. A moment later it was gone, but it soon returned, so I took it upon myself to investigate. I walked out to the front yard, and speaking to the couple inside the vehicle, offered a personal walk-through of the house. They accepted, and I was happy to show them the home I had recreated. I knew all the special features incorporated into the functionality of the kitchen and bathroom designs, and I was fully in my element showing every detail. The master bedroom on-suite was not only the first room remodeled, it was one of the nicest. I named it the Venetian Room, designed with arched framework, glass partitions, tiled walls, and impeccably painted walls. It was also the last room I showed them, and I could see the delight in their expressions over the details and various appointments. I stepped back a little so they could get a feel for the space. Then, unexpectedly, the gentleman said, "I would like to make you an offer you can't refuse." I was happy to hear this, and told him, "Well, how about the asking price?" He agreed, and I contacted Carrie to give her the buyer's agent contact information. The following day Carrie called to tell me a 30-day escrow was opened. This meant I only had 30 days to pack the house, locate a place to rent that would take an unemployed tenant, and arrange for movers to get us from this house to our new home.

Carrie showed me and Jesse a two-story townhome in a very nice area of Orange County that had two master bedrooms. It was a perfect layout, and the owners were willing to accept me if I paid an additional two months' rent up front along with a security deposit equal to one month of rent. This would add up to a hefty sum, but with the proceeds from the sale of the house, plus severance pay and unemployment income, I was easily able to comply. Then, in the midst of packing for the move and responding to the home inspection, Jesse and I learned we finally had an appointment scheduled to meet with the liver transplant team at a facility in Los Angeles several miles from our home.

Movers arrived on the morning of June 30, 2006 and by the end of the day I was able to begin setting up the new townhouse well enough to provide Jesse a comfortable place to rest. Then I set about putting in order the rest of our new home, taking breaks to check on and care for Jesse throughout the evening.

CHAPTER 15

Holding On; Letting Go

WE MET WITH THE TRANSPLANT SPECIALIST in Los Angeles in the early afternoon on June 9th for the first of several transplant evaluation appointments scheduled in two-week intervals over a period of three months. Jesse's birth mother had offered to be a liver donor when we first learned Jesse would eventually need a liver transplant years before. Now his older birth siblings also offered to be donors.

The lead doctor who was head of the liver transplant team was confident his team could handle Jesse's case, and so we were hopeful this would be a snap. Blood types were a match, and everything appeared to be falling into place. However, after further evaluation, we were told the condition of Jesse's lungs had degraded so much they would not sustain a liver transplant. Since the pathology causing the fibrosis of his liver was also occurring in his lungs, the vessels around his lungs and esophagus were not capable of receiving the increased blood flow fed to them after a liver transplant. This meant Jesse would need a double-lung transplant in addition to the liver transplant. According to the cardiothoracic transplant team, the organs needed to come from one donor, so that ruled out his birth family. The new dynamics of the situation also meant a much longer wait time, which seemed impossible for Jesse to survive, given his weight loss and inability to keep anything on his stomach. Still, with no other choice, we persisted. We fulfilled every requirement and attended every appointment, always scheduled for 7:30 a.m. And since traffic on the freeways through Los Angeles was so congested no matter the time of day or night, to be certain we arrived on time for appointments Jesse and I would stay at a hotel near the hospital the night before.

The first appointment with the cardiothoracic team was an extensive two-day evaluation. At the end of the first day, feeling a mix of exhaustion and exhilaration, while we each rested on separate beds in our hotel room, we talked about all we understood up to that point about the transplant program. We talked about our hopes and expectations, and as the conversation evolved, we considered the worst-case scenario; organ rejection. And as our discussion evolved, I could hardly believe I was asking Jesse questions about what he wanted for himself if his new organs went into rejection. I felt I needed to know, and yet it was such a tragic feeling listening to myself ask my child who I loved so deeply what he desired in his last hours. I wondered if I was doing a very good job of concealing my shattered heart. I softly gasped for air a few times, and though I did my best to speak smoothly, I hoped he did not notice how choked with sorrow I was, all the while feeling awe-struck by his responses.

It became obvious to me that Jesse had already given a great deal of consideration to the questions I was asking long before I ever entertained such thoughts. His answers were courageous and compassionate as he told me his requests.

> *"These things he said in words. But much in his heart remained unsaid. For he himself could not speak his deeper secret."* ~ Khalil Gibran, The Prophet

Jesse told me that he wanted to be cremated because his body had gone through such a slow deterioration in this life that he did not want the same thing to continue after he died. And when I asked him how he wanted to be remembered and what my thoughts should be if I must be here without him, without hesitation Jesse told me, "I just want you to always remember how close we are." In retrospect, it is interesting to me that he did not say, "How close we *were*" but "how close we *are*." I believe Jesse was giving me a message of comfort on a deeper level, even if he was not fully aware of the profound activity in his words the moment that he said them. And I have continually remembered his request, convinced he was not only referring to how close he and I are eternally, but also how close he and the heavenly hosts who are with him are to me while I remain.

The heavenly realm is ubiquitous. Within and without, closer than we comprehend it is around us, and it is within each of us. It is simply a different dimension that exists at a much higher frequency than this denser, physical realm. This is why most of us do not perceive heaven with our physical senses. This does not mean, however, that the unseen is not real, inter-active, intelligent, and quite near.

CHAPTER 16

Messages and Messengers

JESSE AND I SPENT THE MONTHS of June, July, and August consumed by the demands of the transplant evaluation process. Throughout the various discussions that took place during the appointments it became clear this facility had never actually performed a combined double-lung and liver transplant. The lead doctor of the cardiothoracic team said she planned to consult with a team of doctors at a pediatric hospital located in the mid-Atlantic region, not too far from the properties I owned in Maryland, regarding the protocol for the procedure, and explained that she would be walked through the surgery over the phone. Naturally, Jesse and I felt less confident the more we learned of this facility in Los Angeles, so we agreed to consider other transplant centers willing to accept him into their program, with an emphasis on the transplant center consulting the Los Angeles team.

Since I had accumulated three investment properties located in Denton, on the Eastern Shore of Maryland, just ninety minutes from Philadelphia, Jesse and I believed it would be feasible to relocate to Maryland where we would live in one of the properties I owned; a newly built, spacious single-family dwelling, located an easy driving distance from the area's community college. I told Jesse, now having completed his tenth-grade year, that he could get his GED after we moved to Maryland and continue his education at the college, taking courses he enjoyed at his own pace. He loved the idea, and we often discussed the details of our plans.

ONE PEACEFUL DAY

"There are magnificent and marvelous things upon which to place the attention and when we go there, there is no struggle, no discord, nor battle."
~ *I Am Discourses, Volume 17*

One evening in late August, in the midst of all the activity surrounding the transplant evaluation, Jesse and I went to relax by the pool in the community where we lived. We positioned a couple of chase lounges in the cast of the final warm rays of the day's setting sun, and while we sat talking a dragonfly hovered near us. At first, we were feeling it was too close for comfort, but at the same time we were fascinated by it. Then to our surprise it landed on Jesse's shoulder! I was amazed. I had never seen such a thing. Jesse was frightened of it because of its size, but I felt sure it would not hurt him, so I said, "Jesse, Jesse! Stay very still. It's giving you Energy!" Of course, I didn't really know if it would give him energy. I simply wanted Jesse to experience the dragonfly without being afraid of it. Jesse knew, too, I was just saying it, but he trusted me so much that he did what I asked, even though he was so frightened. And that dragonfly stayed on his shoulder for a few of the longest seconds of Jesse's life, I do believe. It stayed on him long enough for me to take a picture of it, and then flew away.

A few days later Jesse went with me to run errands, and while we drove along, he struck up an enthusiastic conversation, although what he had to say this time seemed quite out of the blue. Nevertheless, I listened carefully as he explained, "You

know Mom, energy can't be destroyed; it only changes form."
He continued explaining this concept to me by describing water
in its different forms, from frozen to liquid and then to a vapor.
It seemed unusual, given the current circumstances, for him to
be so preoccupied with science and to have such enthusiasm for
explaining this idea, going into such depth for me. In fact, Jesse
was having such difficulty by this time he decided he wanted
a port placed for continuous IV nutrition; the same lipids he
received during previous hospitalizations. I believed it was a good
idea, so I arranged the procedure with the CF clinicians which
was scheduled to take place on Wednesday, September 6th.

Labor Day weekend included a visit with my sister Judy living
in Maryland. I recall how lovely Jesse spoke with her while they
talked one evening. He had a contained, intelligent enthusiasm
as he explained to her the details of the transplant evaluations and
the critical nature of all that must be considered. And he went into
fine detail describing the eco-system he planned to design once
we moved to Maryland. He spoke to her as a mentor, a friend,
and an equal, exuding dignity and grace with each intonation,
in every chosen word, in his poise, his gestures, and his entire
demeanor. My heart was completely moved as I silently observed
from across the room, not daring to interrupt or interject, because
I did not want to disturb the beauty of the scene I was beholding.
I loved him so deeply, and even more as I absorbed every word
and gesture in my quiet amazement.

CHAPTER 17

Tell Me, Wisdom, What Are All These Things?

Author: Kahlil Gibran

"My soul preached to me and taught me to listen to the voices which the tongue and the larynx and the lips do not utter. My soul preached to me and taught me to say, 'I Am ready'..." ~ Kahlil Gibran

ON THE EVENING OF MONDAY, SEPTEMBER 4th Jesse and I drove my sister to the airport in Long Beach for her return flight to Maryland. I spent the following day making the usual preparations for Jesse's planned in-hospital procedure scheduled to take place the following day. As I went through the motions, I had a bitter, unshakeable gut feeling that this time things would not go smoothly for him, but what exactly was going to go wrong I could not discern. All other admissions and the many procedures performed had gone fine, with the exception of course, of the constant annoying interruptions day and night by hospital staff. I also did not know how to explain to Jesse, based on absolutely no tangible evidence and no logical proof, that I was certain this time things would be different and that I did not want him to have the procedure he deemed so necessary, at least not at this particular time. I considered my choices and the only one that seemed reasonable to me was that I trust God to lead us through the upcoming experience.

I gathered a load of laundry and decided to wash a little stuffed Dalmatian puppy we named Ruben. Jesse was two years old when I brought Ruben home one evening after work, and this little stuffed animal was with Jesse from that time on, never leaving his side at home or during hospital stays. I tried to shake the feeling that things were not going to go well during the procedure to place the port, but nothing was working. In fact, the situation worsened when I took Ruben out of the washer. To my utter despair, Ruben was not in the same condition as when he went into the washer. Instead, Ruben's head was completely detached from the little body except for one thread right in the middle of the back of the neck. And what made this whole scenario even more surreal was that none of the stuffing was missing! It was the most overwhelming feeling of panic and despair I had ever experienced. There was no doubt in my entire being this was a sign that Jesse was leaving very soon, but I could not reconcile how Cystic Fibrosis would affect his brain. The most desperate feeling clung like a thick, dark shroud around my heart.

Quietly, while Jesse rested in his room, I frantically searched for a sewing needle and a spool of white thread, and in my shattered and frightened silence I sat secretly in the living room sewing Ruben back together as seamlessly as possible, making small, tightly bound stitches over and over again, hoping it would make a difference somehow, and never mentioning a word to Jesse about any of this.

The following day we entered the hospital and went through the usual long process of admission. Finally, Jesse was taken into the operating room for what should have been a fairly simple procedure, but it did not turn out that way; not by any stretch of the imagination. The plan was to place the port in Jesse's left upper arm because he didn't have enough tissue on his chest to hold the port in place. He was intubated while under sedation, and during the procedure the surgeon noticed blood in the tubing of the respirator. After the procedure was completed the surgeon had Jesse taken to Pediatric ICU. He was kept sedated for two entire days while the pulmonary doctor of the CF clinic tried to figure out why Jesse was bleeding from his lungs. This had been going on for over five years due to the inhaled medications he had been prescribed years prior, and even though I kept telling the doctors and nurses tending to him how to stop the lung bleeds, my words fell on deaf ears.

At times, I thought how easily I might lose him. Watching him from the foot of his bed I sensed I was being shown what it would be like in the end, and I found myself wondering within my heart to God when the end would come. I first thought one year, but then I just needed to believe two years, because I could not imagine him leaving so soon. Once Jesse was finally stabilized and released to a private room, the diminished activity offered us the chance to relax a little. It was a quiet evening, and while he rested, I went to a Starbucks across the street from the hospital to get us both something to sip. While waiting for our order I browsed the items for sale throughout the café and noticed a little-book version of The Velveteen Rabbit. It had been many years since I'd read it and I had only a vague memory of the story line, so I decided to purchase it along with our order.

When I returned to Jesse's room, I nestled the much-loved Ruben comfortably in Jesse's arm and pulled a chair close to his bed where I opened the small book and began to read aloud. As the story progressed, I realized the analogy to Jesse's journey and began to substitute references to The Velveteen Rabbit to *The Velveteen Ruben*. But Jesse and I both knew it was not The Velveteen Ruben either. It was really *The Velveteen Jesse*. My precious Jesse David was becoming real. It seemed to be out of our hands. It seemed to be happening at the speed of light, and nothing I could do would stop it.

Heartbroken, I desperately wanted to hold him and never

let him out of my arms. I tried to disguise my sorrow, but I was certain he felt it, too. Once I finished the story, I held him close and whispered softly, "I love you Jesse David." That was the only thing I was certain would last beyond this life; the love that gave us to each other and instilled in us the strength and courage we had come to master so well; a love that bound us without breach.

CHAPTER 18

Letters to a Friend

JESSE WAS RELEASED FROM THE HOSPITAL after seven days, still weak but we were hopeful that in time the IV nutrition would help him gain more strength and much needed weight.

Seven months prior, in February 2006, at the onset of the downturn Jesse had been experiencing, I began to assert upon the hospital social worker that Jesse deserved a Make-A-Wish for all he had endured. His wish was granted and set to take place over the course of four days beginning on September 13, 2006, just one day after his release from the hospital for the placement of the port. The activity of the prior week was exhausting for both of us. I had very little rest the entire time, but we had come through too much to miss this opportunity, and I was determined to make this special day happen for Jesse as planned. However, I was not aware of just how great a toll the prior week had taken on me.

Jesse was discharged on Tuesday with a regimen that included IV nutrition administered in one-liter quantities over eight hours each day, and a three-week course of intravenous antibiotics administered three times daily. Once home, we managed to get as much rest as possible that night, and the following day, September 13th, a limousine arrived at our home to take us to Universal Studios in Los Angeles for a four-day, three-night stay at the Sheraton Hotel. The following day we were escorted again by limousine from the hotel to the set of the TV show "House M.D." for Jesse's Make A Wish event. All the actors, crew, and staff working on taping the show treated Jesse with enthusiasm and welcomed us on the very busy set. Jesse was well admired by everyone.

After the Make-A-Wish event, I shared our experience by email with several people who kept an interest in Jesse's progress and well-being, and in return I received a few responses from the recipients of my email. I've included a few email exchanges here simply because they offer candid details of not only Jesse's Make-A-Wish, but the events leading up to it.

Date: September 17, 2006
To: Group
Subject: A Wish fulfilled for Jesse David

Hello All,

Several months ago, we learned that Jesse would be the recipient of a Wish granted by the Make-A-Wish Foundation, and on Thursday, September 14th, Jesse's Wish was granted. I'm writing to share with each of you just how his amazing Wish unfolded.

I would like to begin by expressing how very special the Make-A-Wish Foundation made this event for Jesse. Time will never diminish the experience in our hearts and memory.

On Wednesday Jesse and I were escorted a short distance from our home in Anaheim Hills, California, to Los Angeles by limousine to the Sheraton Universal City Hotel where we arrived at 3 p.m. Since we were both recuperating from the activity of his recent hospital stay, released on a regimen that included daily IV nutrition as well as a course of IV antibiotics, we spent the remainder of our first day relaxing at the hotel. Jesse and I ordered up room service for dinner and we thoroughly enjoyed the salmon and fillet mignon! We kicked back during the evening and rested up for Jesse's actual Wish Day event scheduled to begin the following morning at 9:30 a.m. when we were escorted again by limo and taken to Fox Studios where Jesse would encounter his Wish.

On the set of the television show HOUSE M.D. Jesse was able to watch the taping of one of the upcoming third-season episodes. He was first met by the star of the show Dr. House himself, Hugh Laurie. This was so special! Taking time from his truly busy schedule Mr. Laurie made a surprise entrance, approaching Jesse from behind through a doorway leading onto the set of Cuddy's office. He walked over and introduced himself, shook Jesse's hand and then sat with Jesse for several minutes talking about the story in the episode they were taping that day. He also explained that he was still speaking in his American accent because it was too difficult to go back and forth between his British accent and his American accent.

We took a few photos, and Mr. Laurie ran over and grabbed his cane for Jesse to use as a prop for the photos. Jesse loved that! Afterward we were taken to view the taping which had already begun much earlier that morning, and Jesse was seated directly behind the Director. We watched and listened to the taping of the scene, which took several hours, and whenever there was a break or a cut, Mr. Laurie, the Director, and others working on the set would ask Jesse if he thought what they had taped was good enough to print. Jesse always gave a thumbs up.

Between taping the two scenes worked on that day many other members of the cast and crew came to meet and talk with Jesse. The entire staff and crew were very engaging and seemed sincerely happy to have Jesse there. Von, one of the boom operators, kept Jesse entertained, talking with him over the closed mic and headset he and Jesse wore, explaining various aspects of his job. He was telling jokes and prompting Jesse for his opinion about what was happening on set.

Jesse also met several of the office staff in the Art Department and Casting Department. These ladies and gentlemen were thrilled to talk with Jesse and were simply enthralled with the conversation Jesse held with them. By the time we left Jesse had contact information and invitations from several people asking him to stay in touch with them.

What did we learn about the behind the scenes? Well, suffice to say, some very impressive things. Jesse's original wish was to be *on* the show, however, he's glad now that his wish was modified, and here is why. Mr. Laurie took the opportunity to sit with Jesse on the occasions when he had a break from taping and explained that a single show is taped in only eight days. On the day we visited the set we were there for six hours and watched while just one scene took at least four hours to tape. First, several takes were taped from one angle, and then all over again from another angle. And what we found most amazing is that the scenes are only about thirty seconds long! Jesse was quite impressed with the amount of work it takes to create each episode. We also learned that the extras for each show are cast only eight days prior to the start of taping and sometimes the guest actors are not cast until one day before taping begins!

Jesse was intrigued while touring various sets for the show. He saw Cuddy's office, the office of Dr. House, and the various hospital rooms, complete with authentic equipment which included an MRI machine – minus the working parts inside to avoid accidents.

At the end of our visit Jesse was presented with some very special gifts. These included several personally autographed photos of each of the actors and a full DVD set of the second season of the show. He was also presented with an autographed copy of the script of the final episode of the second season and a baseball cap with the title of the show written on the front that he was told to keep very secret from the crew and staff because a very limited number of them were made.

Jesse loved his day! On Friday we hung out at the City Walk. Jesse bought a few souvenirs with the cash gift he was provided by Make-A-Wish and we had lunch at one of the finer restaurants.

Thanks, with all our hearts to Make-A-Wish Foundation for making this a truly special day for Jesse David.

Patricia and Jesse David

Soon afterward I receive responses telling me how nice it was to hear of Jesse's special day. Several people expressed to me how highly they think of the Make-A-Wish Foundation and thanked me for enlightening them to all that goes into taping an episode of one of their own favorite shows. However, one response in particular not only described their awe of Jesse as well as his experience, it went on to share their own close encounter with the Make-A-Wish Foundation when they had recently attended a Tim McGraw and Faith Hill concert. I read the story of a little girl (about twelve years old) who happened to be sitting next to my friend's party of two. She had just experienced her own wish fulfilled during rehearsals before the concert, which was to sing with Faith; which she did during a rehearsal.

It was such a beautiful story that my friend conveyed as he told of the young girl's excitement, and how her eyes were as big as the moon telling them how thrilled she was to have her wish, and how kind Faith and Tim were to her and her parents. As I read on, the emotional effect these things had on my friend was undeniable, not only over the little girl's experience, but also my and Jesse's. My friend wrote that it was finally clear to him that the true gifts in life are the people who touch our lives, and the relationships that are ours to cherish. In his closing comments, my friend expressed that certainly I must leave out a lot of the day to day difficulties, but that Jesse, and others like him, had touched more lives simply by the way he dealt with his day-to-day struggles than most people have in perhaps their entire lifetime.

> *"You have to keep breaking your heart until it opens."*
> ~ *Rumi*

Reading this response was certainly moving. As I absorbed the words and expressions, I felt humbled to be trusted with such sincerity. In my life there have been few occasions when such open trust was apparent. My friend was correct, too. I *did* leave out a lot. In fact, I had become skilled at keeping such things to myself, partly because I was living every parent's worst fear, and few were brave enough to so much as come close to my life, much less embrace it in a manner of friendship. I understood and harbored no grudge or regret, however, having little or no social circle sets the stage in one's life for isolation. I was beginning to recognizing the effect of that in my life at that time, and while on the one hand I was concerned for myself and my wellbeing emotionally, I was, nevertheless, determined to handle this reality in a positive manner. I also understood that our daily life was beyond most people's comprehension, and I seldom divulged such details, even when I had an opportunity to do so. This time, however, I sensed a level of receptiveness and compassion that seemed to offer a permission to do just that. My reply left little to the imagination as I explained the week leading up to Jesse's Make-A-Wish and all I had in deed intentionally left out of my first email. My friend took it quite hard, and replied once more that he had to prepare for a meeting in the office, but first had to pull himself together.

I thought that perhaps I had shared too much too honestly, and something inside of me was sorry I had. But I forgave myself, because up to this point, there were so very few compassionate witnesses to my and Jesse's life, and I needed someone to know; not someone to pity me or Jesse, but someone who cared, as if putting our life and our love and all of our tries for Jesse's life on record, even if miles away the only thing they were able to do was hold that record in their hands and simply read it. And so, I wrote.

Date: September 18, 2006
Subject: Re: A Wish fulfilled for Jesse David

My dear friend, it is difficult to find the words to express how much it meant to me to read your reply, beginning with that little girl singing with Faith Hill and how excited she was about it. These people such as Faith and the crew of House may not fully realize what a legacy they are leaving behind them. It is a gift that will last into eternity; one that I hope comes back to each of them a hundred-fold.

Yes, I leave out quite a lot most times. I don't know what drives me to be honest. It is something much bigger than me, I am sure of that. But I do love Jesse so deeply, and if I can capture or conjure up any good out of this life and hand it to him on a silver platter, I will do just that!

The week prior to his Wish event Jesse was admitted to the hospital. Although it was by choice, he was quite run down and needed to go in. He was down to ninety pounds again and his nausea issues had come on again full-blown, just the way they did back in December and January.

He ended up in Pediatric ICU for two days. During placement of a port, Jesse was intubated because he began coughing while under sedation and he was not recovering easily. The surgeon then became concerned when he saw blood in the tube. Based on his description I had a peace of mind and heart that Jesse would be fine once the tube was removed, but instead he was kept intubated and sent to P-ICU to recover. He kept bleeding though, every time he coughed, and it was the most pathetic sight.

Over a twenty-four-hour period, Jesse lost at least 400cc of blood, and the longer I watched this go on, the more I was convinced I would be leaving that place without him. I'm not sure how I stayed sane through it all. He looked so terrible and I had no sleep for two and a half days. It was constant activity; if there was one of the ICU staff at his bed, there were four or five.

I was with him the entire time, and each time the nurses saw blood in the tube they looked to me to tell them whether the bleeding was fresh or from a prior cough and bleed. I wrote that off to my own experience with Jesse and my familiarity with these incidents. He started having bleeds when he was ten years old, a degradation caused by one of the inhaled medications he was prescribed, and though he has not been on it for a few years now, the damage is done and he is still prone to bleeding from his lungs.

Through it all Jesse ended up needing two pints of blood, two bags of platelets, and a bag of plasma to stabilize him. About sixteen hours into this whole scenario I told the ICU staff if the doctor (who wanted to check his lungs by way of the tube for areas that may need to be sealed off) was later than 9:00 a.m., I wanted the tube removed.

The PICU staff kept trying to stop the bleeding with various medications, but nothing was working. The doctor arrived at 8:30 a.m. the following morning, and I watched as he tried every method that he had at his disposal to stop the bleeding from Jesse's lungs. Once he was finally completely exasperated by his attempts, I decided to risk my credibility once again, as I had when I introduced Glutathione to Jesse's natural regimen. I told him that I have a simple method for stopping these bleeds instantly with oral supplements of the amino acid L-Lysine. He said he would "welcome anything that would work, even if it is alternative and to go home and get the stuff!"

This doctor used the ventilation tube to check Jesse's lungs with a telescopic lens while Jesse was still under sedation. Once the procedure was completed Jesse was removed from the ventilator and within moments there were no more bleeding episodes. That is what I tried to explain to the P-ICU staff all along, and though it took two days, they were finally witness to what I considered the obvious. But I must share, the experience of those two days gave me a preview of what it will be like at the end, and I began to prepare my heart and mind for that.

Jesse is so amazing. He was kept sedated the entire time he was intubated, and when he came to after being extubated and realized he had missed two whole days of his life he sobbed. I realized even more so how important each day and every hour are to him, especially now. He wants to be aware of every moment he is living, for obvious reasons. At first, I tried to console him by telling him all that had occurred and why. Then I remembered the pad of paper at the foot of his bed. It had several pages of notes he wrote while sedated. You see, occasionally his blood pressure would drop, and the nurses would let up on the sedation just enough to stabilize him. During those few short minutes Jesse would come to a groggy state of awareness and try to do everything from stand up to go to the bathroom, to demand certain things be done "right now!" Since he was intubated and could not speak, I gave him a pad of paper and pencil. His very first words were "I'm nacked!" Of course, this was not a time for levity, but I had to crack a grin over his strength of determination and survival instinct, not to mention the way he spelled "naked." He kept coming back to the fact that he had no boxers on beneath his hospital gown. It was just too undignified for him. It is certainly sad when a person has little left to cling to but their right to their own dignity, and in those moments, Jesse was feeling that being taken from him. I don't think I ever heard him complain about the multitude of things he faced daily over the years he's lived, until then.

Well, he had written on perhaps fifteen pages front and back, and when I handed the pad of paper to him, he took it from me eagerly and read those notes over and over again, flipping through the pages front and back several times, trying to absorb everything, I believe so he could make those two missing days as real a memory as possible.

It seems this life of mine is so tragically privileged. On the one hand, I cannot fathom the sorrow and suffering of it all, and on the other hand, I feel humbled to be trusted by Heaven above with such an awesome responsibility; to be trusted to care for a child who is suffering through every day he lives! To be responsible for loving and comforting him as much as he deserves to be and needs to be is a privilege in its own right. But I never imagined I would be able to do what I am doing. Truly, I am facing my own worst fears, and somehow, I'm not crumbling. I was always so afraid of having to watch Jesse suffer. And it does so tear my heart to shreds when I have time to ponder any of this. But there is this other thing in me that seems to be cushioning me through this experience, and sort of leading me. Somehow, without fail, I am prepared for each new phase and the experiences we encounter. And even though I so often feel like I'm facing a brick wall looking for answers to the problems he's living with, somehow Jesse and I get to the next place and phase, and sometimes we find just a little reprieve or unexpected kindness that seems like Christmas to a five-year-old.

The week prior to going into the hospital we both slept straight through two nights in a row without any episodes. That was a first since December 2005. But he was feeling so poorly from the weight he's lost that for a couple of weeks I had him sleep in my bed with me. I have a big king size sleigh bed that made it easy for him to sleep propped up, which is how he has been sleeping since December. I put a pillow between us for his comfort and was able to rub his head and arms to help him sleep more peacefully. He is just so frail I have been worrying over how long he will last this way, so I decided to keep him as near as possible without causing him discomfort. You know, at sixteen and a half years old he looks like he is about twelve years old right now. He's lost so much weight, and although his color is pretty good, his frame is quite small due to the nutritional deficiencies over the past several years. But he has such a beautiful face that people often mistake him for being a girl. Yeah, all the time! So, I gave it some thought, and I believe I have an answer for that. I think that when people, especially children, who go through such hardship they eventually begin to take on the beauty of angels' faces, however most of us don't recognize that. Like the little girl who was telling you about her Wish with Faith Hill. I imagine she was so beautiful despite anything apparent she may have been showing of her illness.

In closing, today I sent off Jesse's medical records for the past year to a hospital located about ninety minutes from the house I own in Maryland. My plan is to relocate us some time in December just in time for Jesse to have a great Christmas with my family. It is time, I feel, to get us out of isolation. I am alone here, and I am realizing I will need them in the not-too-distant future.

Thank you sincerely for writing.

Patricia

CHAPTER 19

The Length of Love

Once home from the Make-A-Wish event we had only one extremely difficult week together before Jesse entered the hospital again - for the last time. I was exhausted, completely run down. Over the years, with each new phase and increased level of activity concerning Jesse's progression and all that was required to properly care for him, I was now at a place where I was able to function on segments of sleep, capturing two or three hours during the day and throughout the night when Jesse was comfortable and also able to rest. On a day-to-day basis I never noticed if I felt tired or run down, but this time I felt quite different. I was nauseous and had the worst headache I had ever experienced. I was never prone to headaches and this one was profoundly painful. And since Jesse was prone to migraines, it troubled me to think he might come down with the same symptoms if what I had was something contagious.

On Monday morning I came face to face with what I feared when Jesse began to exhibit the same symptoms I had, but even more severe than my own. He had a follow-up appointment scheduled for early Wednesday morning with the pulmonary clinic. They would be checking his progress with the port, and since we were familiar with flu symptoms, we waited for that appointment. I had him sleep in my bed Monday and Tuesday nights so I could tend to him more quickly, because I was still so exhausted and concerned that I would not be able to respond to him soon enough if we were in different bedrooms.

By Tuesday night Jesse was in a great deal of discomfort. Throughout the first few hours of the night we both drifted in and out of a restless sleep, during which I fell into two terribly frightening dreams. The dreams seemed to be signaling not only that we had approached the end of Jesse's life, but also how it would happen for him. The first dream was of Jesse and me drowning in a flood. The second dream involved a very small and meticulously sculpted stone carving that one of Jesse's birth brothers called an orb. He had handcrafted it himself, and gave as a gift to Jesse just two months earlier during one of the transplant evaluation appointments. From the moment I laid eyes on it, it seemed to resonate an energy of its own, as if it actually existed consciously. I felt fascinated by the intricate details that depicted a face half human-half beast, while also feeling repelled by my sense that it had some other-worldly origin and mission. Indeed, it seemed to fulfill its purpose when, I watched in my dream as a drill of proportionate size extracted at least four very small circular cores from the head of the beast which silently and motionlessly submitted to the process. I was horrified by the scene and woke up gasping for air, reaching for Jesse to be sure he was still with me and still breathing. I looked at the clock. Two-thirty a.m. Exhausted, I fell back into a lucid sleep, while holding on to Jesse's arm across the pillows nestled between us.

Around 3:15 a.m. Jesse's pain had reached an all-time peak. He asked me to help him into his own bedroom where he could watch TV. Had I only thought to lay down with him in his bedroom, I could have stayed close to him for a few hours longer, but I was too exhausted to realize it at the time. I gathered the IV feed and helped him walk to his room just a few feet across a short hallway. He found a place to sit on the floor to the left and slightly behind me while I worked to place several pillows and a sheet on the couch that had been his bed for nearly a year by this time which allowed him to rest in an inclined position. I kept turning around to make sure he was still there, still sitting wrapped in the small blue knit blanket he clutched tightly around his small frame.

Jesse David at a transplant evaluation appointment holding the Orb his birth-brother Jeremiah made for him.

LOOK WHAT HAPPENS WITH A LOVE LIKE THAT

"Even after all this time the sun never says to the earth,
'you owe me'. Look what happens with a love like that.
It lights the whole sky."
~ Hafiz

As I worked quickly to arrange the pillows and sheet, Jesse suddenly spoke out in a tone and strength of voice I found surprising, given his weak and pain-wracked state of being. He told me, "I really lucked out!" A swirl of reactions came over me, and although I believed I knew what he meant, I asked him, "Jesse, why are you saying that?" He said, "Because look at all you do for me. Look at how you're always there for me." My awe as I listened to him could not be measured. I told him I was simply doing everything I should do; moreover, it was everything I wanted to do for him. I could not begin to quantify my profound love for him and my desire that his life had been so very different from what he experienced.

Once he was resting, propped up by pillows behind him and under his slender arms for support, I returned to my own bedroom and fell asleep from sheer exhaustion. I awoke less than three hours later, at 6:00 a.m., startled to have slept so long without checking on Jesse. I rushed into his room to see if he was all right, thankful to find him awake and breathing! I freshened myself and then helped him dress, brush his teeth, and comb his hair. I helped him into the car and drove us to the clinic for the appointment we were both now so much in need of.

When we arrived at the facility, I let Jesse out of the car in front of the main doors and told him I would meet him in the lobby of the building near the elevators. He was in too much pain to walk the distance from the parking lot to the clinic, and though I had introduced the idea of a wheel chair for him on a couple occasions, he consistently refused, perhaps because it would have been too great an indicator of his decline. But while on our way to the clinic he told me he decided he wanted to discuss getting a wheelchair with the clinician.

I circled the lower level of the parking garage closest to the building, but found no open spaces, so I drove to the next parking level. I grabbed a space near the steps leading down to the street level and ran to make my way into the facility. I looked for Jesse, expecting to see him sitting on one of the benches positioned near the elevators, but he wasn't there. I scanned the lobby, but he was nowhere in sight. A feeling of desperation consumed me. Hoping to find him at the clinic a couple floors up, I waited at the elevator, my heart pounding with overwhelming worry. It seemed to take an eternity for the doors to open and then finally reach the second floor.

When I stepped out of the elevator a short distance from the entrance to the clinic I looked frantically for Jesse. I found him sitting on a bench a few feet from the entrance to the clinic. He was pale and weak. I noticed he had slipped his shoes off for some reason. I hurried to where he was sitting, and as I approached him, I realized he was having a strange kind of difficulty slipping his feet back into his shoes. He seemed to have no coordination, even though he knew what he wanted to do. I had never seen him act that way. It simply was not like him, and my concern was deepening every second.

Once inside the clinic we were immediately taken to an exam room. Jesse began speaking to the clinic RN about his decision for a wheelchair, but a few minutes into the discussion it became difficult for him to express his thoughts. The doctor entered the exam room and at once recognized Jesse's unusual behavior and inability to communicate. He asked Jesse a series of simple questions to assess his symptoms, and even while the doctor asked his questions, it became obvious Jesse was declining quickly. Within a few minutes Jesse could not tell us where he was. He had to think about his answers. The only answer he could give to any question was simply his name. A wheelchair was brought into the exam room and the RN and I helped Jesse into it. The hospital was notified, and we rushed to get him across the parking lot to the hospital where he was admitted under emergency. Shortly thereafter, he was provided a private room in the Pediatric Intensive Care Unit.

CHAPTER 20

Just A Little Longer

OVER THE NEXT FEW HOURS, I held him in my arms, interjecting information to the doctors and nurses tending to him. Amid everything happening I recalled a long-forgotten lullaby I made up for him when he was just a few weeks old, personalized with all my love for him. It came back to me in those moments as clearly as if I had never forgotten it, and I began singing it to him. Jesse's ability to communicate continued to decline steadily, and when he could no longer speak, he began using his eyes to answer simple questions; up and down for Yes, and left and right for No.

As it turned out, Jesse's symptoms were characteristic of encephalopathy due to kidney failure. The patient knows what they want to say, but a certain word or phrase becomes fixed in the brain activity and it becomes the only response the patient is able to give. Whenever we would ask Jesse questions to assess his decline, I could see the saddest, most puzzled look on his face when he could only say his name. Though what has always amazed me, and puzzled the doctors, is that whenever I said, "I love you Jesse David" he would always reply, "I love you too, Mom."

Through it all it was obvious we were connected on a deeper level, and even as his communication diminished, I knew instantly every change in his method to answer questions. Finally, knowing that soon I would never have another chance to speak to him, I asked him one final question. "Jesse, do you want to get better?" I watched for his answer, but he could no longer move his eyes up and down or left and right. Then I saw it! He raised his eyebrows very high, giving a firm demand in the positive. Yet, I felt certain somehow that he knew, as did I, this time things were not going to turn around for us. I thought perhaps he was giving me an affirmative gesture to let me know he loved me enough to try that hard. Nevertheless, regardless of his reasons, and perhaps regardless of his answer, I needed to give him every chance, every method and means to come back to me, and I was determined to exhaust every measure for his sake.

As the hours passed all too quickly, I held my precious Jesse David in my arms and watched as he drifted further and further away from me. Then, in the early hours of the evening, the attending doctors told me Jesse David was in a state of kidney failure. It was not long afterward I would never again hear his precious voice speak to me; never again would I gaze into the eyes that held my heart a willing captive.

Date: September 28, 2006 12:18 a.m.
To: Group

Jesse David is in P-ICU. He is in acute kidney failure. He is incoherent, unable to comprehend or communicate anything at this time. Until the early morning hours of the night he was only able to say his name, except when I told him I love him; he was able to tell me he loves me, too.

Jesse will be receiving total dialysis treatment daily, beginning today. However, he has many contradictory indications that I am told are uncharacteristic of kidney failure which are not understood at this point.

Jesse is being kept stable under sedation and has been put on a ventilator this morning. His vital issues are being monitored by several means, including extensive blood draws through central lines.

It cannot be determined if Jesse will recover, although when I asked him last night if he wanted to get better, he raised his eyebrows very high.

Patricia

CHAPTER 21

God Keeps His Word

It is said, when we love someone, we wrap them in the Robe of God. This Robe is Light, it is Love, and it is Eternal. This Love animates the body and gives power to the mind. It is the Energy of Life that never dies. It is conscious intelligence that is wise enough to have manifested the physical world and the physical structure. This Love, this Energy of Life that is the real person eternally, is what binds us eternally, because nothing can change the Love of God's Heart.
~ PmCornett

I STAYED WITH JESSE CONSTANTLY THROUGHOUT the days and nights. No matter the procedure ordered for him I was close by, watching every activity; the blood draws, the CAT scans, the dialysis. I stood only a few feet away from his bed and watched while two surgeons worked to place a central line in each of Jesse's upper thighs. I can still see the surgeon who stood on the left side of his bed gently wiping the blood from Jesse's skin where the first of two incisions were made. As I quietly observed the scene, I felt grateful for their efforts and wondered if Jesse could feel my presence near to him and if he knew just how profound was my love for him.

As I gazed upon a face so beautiful and sacred to my heart that the spoken word could not convey the essence of its solemn nature, feeling sad and confused, I could only think that things were not supposed to go this way, and yet they did. He had always pulled through before, but this time felt so different, and I began retracing the magnificent events leading up to this moment, unfolding every detail in sequence, reliving our journey in my mind.

Seventeen years had passed since Jesse's adoptive father and I submitted our adoption resume and completed the interview process. Afterward, with an undetermined length of time to wait, hoping daily to be chosen by a birth mother, I believed the most constructive way to use the time we had would simply be to pray. One evening when I was open to God in a manner that I'd seldom experienced, choosing my words very carefully, I tried to think of the most honorable reason I could pose to God to ensure my prayers would be heard and I would be allowed to be a mother. As I searched my heart, I realized the only thing that could not be denied is love; just love. So, I asked God to give me a child to love. I did not want to make that child like me or have a child for any self-centered reasons. I just wanted to love a child and allow the life entrusted to me to become everything it was meant to be, not by my design, by divine design.

While I prayed in a soft whisper, it was suddenly as if someone took over my voice, just like a radio signal when it interferes with the frequency of another radio signal. The first station fades out and another station cuts in, just as clear as the first. I could scarcely believe what was happening as I listened to the words falling from my lips as gentle and unprovoked as dew from a leaf in the cool of the morning saying, "And I know you will help me with anything that happens."

I was stunned! I became so terribly frightened I honestly did not know what to do. It was not because those words came from my own lips without passing through a conscious thought process.

Nor was it the message that frightened me. I had no doubt God helps everyone with everything that happens. This is a given. What worried me so much was the fact that I was being reminded of it, because there is absolutely no reason that I would need this reminder except that I would find it necessary and useful at some point in time. No one is immune to experiences which, relatively speaking, can seem excruciating, frightening, or tragic. Certainly, my own life was evidence of this, and yet through it all, I was never given such a reminder - until now.

Contemplating what lie ahead was more than I could bear. I tried to laugh it off and thought to myself, "Well, I hope it's just teenage rebellion." But in my heart, I was certain something much greater than I could comprehend at the time was ahead of me. I had no clue what it was, but I knew it was going to be difficult. I knew I was going to face my own worst fears.

In the same moments I realized I had a choice. I could either choose to not be a mother and lose that blessing, or I could convince my mind that what just occurred never actually happened. After considering the implications of each choice for a few minutes, I chose the latter. And I completely forgot the entire incident for a very proper seven years!

Five years later when I received the news of Jesse's diagnosis, I was terrified for myself and for Jesse. I had developed the routine of going for a drive during my lunch hour. During that one hour I was able to break away from the pressures of my job and concentrate on the only thing that really mattered to me; Jesse David. I often cried and prayed while I drove the highways between the office and our home, never really having an intended destination in mind. It was the only time I could find to release the worry pent up inside me, and the only time I cried. I did not entertain such activities at home or around Jesse. I wanted him to feel safe and secure in my ability to care for him. We focused on living; thriving, not suffering.

After nearly two years of this routine, on a particular day as I took to the highway, I felt more overwhelmed than at any other time up to that point. We had just begun a journey that would take years to unfold, and my fear of what lie ahead for Jesse and me, on top of the sorrow I bore, consumed my heart and became every tortured thought of my mind. I felt angry over the cruelty of it all. Within a few minutes I began to lay it on the line with God. I told Him I was not afraid of Him anymore, and since He gave me this, He must help me! I demanded He provide for us, and He must keep me strong! Perhaps above all, He must give me wisdom! Hurling demand after demand, I was just slightly amused because I felt no condemnation whatsoever. I wondered if He was even concerned at all, so I decided to test Him in some way to see if I could get a reaction out of this Entity who, in those moments, seemed to be nothing more than a distant and passive over-seer of our demise. I became firmer, bolder and louder. I began sobbing and ordering God to be all that I needed to take care of Jesse.

Then, in the midst of what had developed into an uncontrolled rant, which to my knowledge was audible to absolutely no one I could actually perceive, other than myself, my words were intercepted – just the way God will do at times when enough is enough – and I heard the most tender reply I could have imagined saying, "And I know you will help me with anything that happens." It came back into my mind like a calm and loving whisper.

These were the precise words that terrified me so thoroughly seven years before which I so efficiently blocked from my memory. If I had realized the first time that I heard them that they were intended for my comfort, and the demands I made in those same moments were already provided for, then I would not have felt a need to forget the reminder He gave so well. But God does not forget. God keeps His Word. And although I was frightened by those words the first time that I heard them from my own lips, this time they were the most comforting words I had ever heard.

I was instantly quieted, hushed into a solemn and reverent

silence. Humbled now, I pondered the incident, drawing out every comfort my mind could conceive. I concluded the only thing left for me to do was to trust God to keep His Word, and while I drove back in the direction of my office, I told God we had an Agreement and I was going to hold Him to it without any more ranting. And I did - and He did.

The two surgeons, still bedside in Jesse's private Pediatric ICU room, were quietly discussing the completed procedure while they placed surgical tape on the site of each incision. I stood there alone, listening to as much as I could hear of their soft-spoken exchange, unaware that what was intended to be a life-saving procedure would soon become the framework for yet another complication.

I was weary from the day, feeling deeply torn in my heart and in my conscious thoughts, yet I was also aware that despite the critical events taking place a peace had also taken hold of me during these final days I had been given with Jesse David that was starkly beyond my own understanding.

CHAPTER 22

The Final Analysis

My birthday came and went, appropriately without recognition, on the second day of Jesse's final week. It was on this day a CAT scan was scheduled to try to determine why Jesse was in such a deep coma. After the procedure was completed, I followed close behind the attendants as they wheeled his bed through the tunnels to take him back to his room in the P-ICU. As we turned the first corner on our trek through the hallways, I saw a shadow that seemed to come from nowhere. I had the strong impression that it was not coincidental, and hoping to resolve my curiosity, I looked around to know who, or what, may have caused it. As I peered behind me, and above at the lights emitting a soft, diffused illumination of the halls, a firm and immoveable peace came over me. I thought that surely God was covering us in the shadow of His wings and the comfort of His Love, while also letting me know it was time for Jesse to leave; that Jesse was, in fact, with God at that very moment. It felt as though God was assuring me of just how much he loves Jesse, explaining to me that it was time for Jesse to come Home. I wondered if God had seen enough suffering for one precious life. What argument did I have that God would listen to this time? Before Jesse was born, I told God I just wanted to love a child. And it seemed that is precisely what God gave me in answer to my prayer. And so, remaining very still in my heart, I quietly returned to God the gift of love He lent to me only a few short years before, my beautiful little crown, my precious Jesse David.

Throughout the next few days Jesse's doctors from the Pulmonary and GI clinics did not seem to recognize me. Certainly, I should be ranting about something or other. I believed they were nervous, wondering if at any moment I would break into a vehement outburst over what was happening to my child. But it never happened. In fact, I was no less puzzled, barely familiar with myself during the events unfolding throughout Jesse's final week. On the one hand, I realized that no level of criticism or any amount of crying and ranting would help ease any of the things Jesse was going through. It would not reverse the kidney failure or bring him out of the coma. Nor would it create an atmosphere of calm for him. This is not to say, however, that I did not have many strong opinions and severe impressions about what should have been done differently throughout the years. I knew from the beginning that Jesse's pathology was not typical. He was not a typical CF, and I had expressed that on many occasions to the doctors who followed Jesse's progress from the time I first received his diagnosis. If only they were more willing to consider my input, my observations on a day-to-day basis. If only they had not clung so tightly to the protocol derived by the facility meant to serve the masses with no flexibility for the specific needs of the individual patient, Jesse David might have thrived many more years. He might have lived the dreams he had for his life. He might have known a love of his own. He might have been able to accomplish the great things he was capable of. And I would have been given more time to look upon his face, listen to his voice, and smile just to hear him laughing. These things would never happen now, and no matter how I felt, it would not change a single thing.

The peace I felt despite those impressions was very nearly surreal, and I was aware of the stranger I had become, not only to everyone who knew me, but to myself as well. It was most uncharacteristic, given the many occasions when I complained about a myriad of issues during clinic visits. I wondered what had happened to the battle I was always fighting. Where was the anger and fear at this crucial point? Instead, the only thing that mattered to me now was the subjugation of any and all obstruction to the profound intelligence required and the compassion I desired for Jesse's life in these critical, final hours. When I think back on it now, I had a sense of being wrapped in a kind of very peaceful energy that allowed me to think clearly and even, dare I say, positively.

On Friday morning the P-ICU resident doctor in charge of Jesse's case throughout the week explained to me that a systemic yeast infection had been detected in Jesse's blood draws. Until then, this same doctor continually assured me they could "fix this thing." He was confident that once the dialysis treatment was started Jesse would come out of the coma and stabilize. Now he had no hope to offer me. He explained that even though treatment was being administered for the yeast infection, there was little chance it would work because it had clustered around every life-saving device that entered his body. There was no way to stop the yeast infection from clinging to those intravenous lines, and that would mean each one of those devices would have to be removed. He then told me to consider contacting anyone I believed would want to see Jesse for the last time.

Listening as this doctor told me they could do no more for Jesse, I found myself grasping for something to believe in that was greater and wiser, more powerful and more compassionate than any of the attempts made for Jesse's life up to this point. And in those few short moments I realized I could do everything for him. I realized I could give him Heaven, and in so doing I knew I could give him even more than I ever imagined for him in this world. It was the greatest gift I could present to him, the ultimate healing and the greater perfection. And in that perfection is the enormous expanse and balance of harmony inherent throughout all eternity, the portion he so greatly deserved, because certainly he had struggled, and much more severely than I ever imagined he would at the start. Yet, through it all he was always so compassionate and loving. He never complained that his life was not good. He never once said he had been dealt a bad hand. Jesse's response to life – his own life and others' – was always only dignity, respect for his own body, and understanding for the people who passed through the few, yet profound years of his sacred, precious life. My beloved Jesse David will never cease to amaze me, because he was wise even in his youth, compassionate despite the difficulties he experienced, courageously enduring every aspect of his experience. And as I watched him go through it all, I held my heart still in order to be strong so that I could teach him how to survive. I wanted him to know how much I love him. I wanted him to live all his hopes and dreams. I wanted to see the man he would become.

Observing him now where he lay throughout his final week, contemplating the enormity of our life together and the profound life Jesse David accomplished, I began to realize I was in fact looking upon the man. Jesse David had become a man while yet in his youth, for certainly the qualities that characterize love, courage, and wisdom were the very things which defined him. In fact, he taught me more about these things than any other experience or mentor I had encountered before him, and he is teaching me still.

After three days lying in the deepest coma with absolutely no brain function, the breathing machine at 100% velocity, failed lungs, failed kidneys, and now fighting a systemic yeast infection, the neurologist told me Jesse was also experiencing strokes on the brain.

I called Jesse's father, who arrived the same day. I had Jesse's phone, so I began searching through his contacts and tried to reach as many of Jesse's friends as I could, as well as the school

Jesse was attending. Perhaps most importantly, I was able to get a message through to Jesse's birth family. Jesse's birth family made the four-hour trip from their home in Visalia to Orange County early the following morning. They stayed close to Jesse from the moment they arrived on Saturday throughout the weekend. We spent time during the first two days reminiscing about the amazing Jesse David we each knew and loved so deeply, and even more so in those final days. Jesse loved his birth family, and for the next two days while they remained close to him, Jesse remained consistently calm. So much so that it was evident to everyone, including the doctors and nurses caring for him, that his birth family's presence was by all means Jesse's peace. On Monday morning they arrived at the hospital for their final visit with Jesse, and each took time to say their good-byes to him before returning to their home.

Carli, Jesse David's cousin, came to visit him. Before she left, she asked for a few moments alone with Jesse. Carli's mother and I walked out of his room and gently closed the door behind us. I was in awe of her. Her mother and I watched through the window in the door of his room as precious Carli, only three years older than Jesse, and never having encountered an event such as what she was experiencing now, stood next to his bed speaking to him while caressing his hand.

Each night I slept next to Jesse David's bed on a small chair that unfolded to a makeshift bed. It was 11:30 p.m. on Monday night, the sixth night into Jesse's final week. I tried to rest. I slept lightly for about two hours, and then I was stirred awake with the unmistakable awareness that God wanted my attention. The message was that I not wait too long. I looked at the clock in the room. It was 1:30 a.m. I struggled throughout the next four hours of the night, lying very still, trying to stay alert to what was being required of me. I asked questions of God and myself, as if I was sifting my very soul like fine sand. I fell back to sleep around 5:30 a.m. and slept for two more hours.

Upon waking at 7:30 a.m. Tuesday morning October 3rd, I requested the charge nurse arrange a meeting with the doctors and specialists assessing Jesse's case. I wanted the Pulmonologists, the Neurologist, a social worker, and any others over-seeing his case to be present. The meeting was scheduled for 11:00 a.m. the same morning. In the meantime, I went home to shower. The struggle within me continued. My conversation with God the night before was not concluded. I knew He was insisting I not hold Jesse David longer than necessary, but I needed to be sure of when to let him go. I needed to be sure I was really following God's instructions, and just as important, that I was complying with Jesse's desires.

I struggled within my heart and mind to come to terms with every aspect of the decisions I was faced with, including my own motives and the timing of his leaving. I stared at myself in the mirror while cleaning my face and combing my hair, wondering what to base anything of these decisions on. I hardly recognized the face peering back at me. I knew only two things for sure. First, the love this child drew forth from my beating heart was more than could be quantified. And second, I would be eternally accountable for every move, motive, and choice I made for this sacred, precious life trusting me, depending on me now, just as he had all the days of his life, to do exactly what he needed, exactly as *he* desired for his life.

While I considered these things, searching the depths of my soul and calling out to the heights of heaven Itself, I remembered something my youngest sister, Gina, said to me the day before: "God won't *let* you make a wrong decision for Jesse." And at that very moment I realized God was in complete control, even over me. In fact, He had been in control the entire time Jesse had been in my life. I recalled the words that came from my own lips years before. The same words that came back to me seven years later, "I know You will help me with anything that happens." In the same fleeting moments, I began to realize that God, Jesse, and his birth mother had trusted me from the very start with Jesse's life. Perhaps what amazed me most was realizing God knew all of this before Jesse was even born. And as these realizations became clearer, I found myself the recipient of a trust so magnificent I could hardly believe I was the one chosen to be Jesse's mother, chosen to care for and love a life as delicate and profound as Jesse's life had been.

I pondered these things, calling for more of God's wisdom, more of His courage and His divine love sustained within my recognition. I believed if God, Jesse, and his birth mother trusted me with Jesse's life, then I was also being trusted with his transition. That is when I began to trust myself to make the right decision for Jesse. Then I recounted the conversation Jesse and I had during the transplant evaluations. When I asked him how he wanted things to unfold if his new organs went into rejection and we knew he had little time left, he told me he just wanted everyone to be peaceful. He didn't want a lot of crying and confusion about the circumstances. And so, I believed that was a place to begin navigating the crucial events that would put in motion the next phase of the profound life we had experienced; one that would last eternally.

When I returned to the hospital the neurologist was examining Jesse. I met her in his room and stood quietly watching his responses to the tests she performed to determine Jesse's level of brain activity. She explained to me that Jesse had no brain function except for what the brain stems produce, and there was evidence that even this small amount of function was diminishing quickly. Within moments I was led inside the meeting room, just a few feet away from the room where Jesse David quietly lay. The neurologist continued explaining to me her conclusions of the examination she performed just minutes before. I listened, heart-broken, as she told me there was strong evidence Jesse David was also having strokes on his brain, the number and severity of which were not able to be determined. She admitted there was no clinical reason she could determine for why Jesse had gone into such a deep coma, and she was certain that even if they were able to bring him out of the coma, which had already been attempted in various ways, the damage done to his brain would reveal no trace of the personality characterizing the child-man I had always known. He would have no mobility and no awareness whatsoever of his surroundings. Nor would he know me. Then one of the pulmonologists spoke up, adding to this tragic prognosis by explaining that Jesse's condition also meant that now he could not be considered a candidate for transplant.

I asked the group of specialists in the meeting what steps would be taken when I decided it was time to let Jesse go. They explained the details, assuring me Jesse would be kept comfortable, sedated, and pain-free. Once I had answers to all the questions I could think of, I requested one thing more of each person present in the meeting, saying, "I know you cannot give me any hope that Jesse David will recover, but I would like to know as much about him as I can. I am asking each of you to tell me something about him, no matter what it is. I simply want to know all I can about him before I let him go." I listened as each one said a few words. Some spoke regarding his medical condition, and others regarding their admiration of him. Jesse's regular team of doctors took this opportunity to assure me I had done everything possible for Jesse, and that because of my efforts Jesse lived longer than he would have been expected to. I found little comfort in those words, however. I knew very well my efforts for this precious life. I knew the love that drove me, and I believed Jesse did too. All my love, all my tries for his life seemed too sacred for them to speak of. I simply stared back at them, wishing this same team of doctors had listened to my pleas over the years leading up to this tragic day.

CHAPTER 23

Final Hours

TWO OF THE NURSES WHO TENDED to Jesse throughout his final week requested they be scheduled to care for him during his final hours. As the remainder of the day and evening progressed, I was aware of their deliberate careful and quiet attention to his every need. I could see the compassion they felt for him, yet they kept their composure, as if they knew instinctively Jesse David wanted a peaceful calm about his leaving.

Jesse David was usually ready to rest at the same time each evening, 9:00 p.m., so I requested arrangements to be made for the same time on this particular evening to allow me to give him his leave. It was time for my Jesse David to rest his precious soul.

At 6:00 p.m. his daytime nurse, Angela, and I began preparations. We carefully washed Jesse's precious body. I gently wiped his face and combed his thick, golden-brown, shoulder-length hair. Nurse Angela asked if I wanted a lock of his hair. We carefully cut a lock from an area where it would not show, in case he was to care. Once finished cleansing him, the G-tube was removed from his tummy and a bandage placed over the opening. Within a few minutes the respiratory therapist entered the room and carefully removed him from the ventilator. I watched as he worked, hoping Jesse would not go into a coughing spell. To my comfort he was undisturbed by the change. During each phase of preparation, it seemed I was being given every assurance that Jesse was at peace with my decision for him.

Jesse was made comfortable in his bed, and with the help of his nurse, I carefully situated myself in the bed next to him and gently placed my left arm under him to cradle him close to me. Nurse Angela entered the room every few minutes to check on us, and sometimes she administered more of the medication that kept Jesse sedated and pain-free.

Andrew, Jesse's friend who often visited him during his hospitalizations, insisted he wanted to be with Jesse now. He sat in a chair pulled close to the left side of the bed, holding and caressing Jesse's hand, while hiding his tear-soaked face in his own arm resting on the bed. He cried silently, looking up every few minutes to glance at me and to look upon Jesse's face. I watched, helpless to relieve his grief as he searched for Jesse's response to his love for him.

While holding Jesse David in my arms I spoke to him of things I hoped would comfort him. I told him how much I love him, and how proud I am of him. As the minutes passed, I listened to his shallow breaths. They were as rhythmic and deliberate as the beating of our hearts, his and mine, and while I spoke to him, he seemed to love the sound of every word and expression of my love for him. I thought about the times I would sing to him at night when I tucked him into bed. He would ask me to "sing that song again", or "sing another song, Mom."

Every few minutes I glanced at the stats on the monitor situated high on the wall to the left side of his bed. There was only silence as the numbers declined, and when I was sure they could go no lower, I told my precious Jesse David, "This is not good-bye. I will see you soon." Although, just like the words that came from my lips before he was born, I did not intend to say, "I will see you *soon*." The words I intended to say were, "I will see you *again*." I was startled when I heard myself say the word *soon*, but I was also comforted. I felt very good, in fact, because I wanted to go with him right then. I never thought twice about it. It simply seemed the natural thing to do. After all, we had always been together.

In that moment, with those final words, Jesse David let go. It was all so beautiful; tragic beyond any expression I know of, yet beautiful somehow. He went through that last hour so peacefully, as if he wanted it. Somehow, I didn't cry. I was terrified, but I didn't cry, because I could not disregard his request that everything and everyone be calm. And so, I held myself peaceful while I held him in my arms.

FAREWELL IS NOT GOOD-BYE

Now, Jesse's friend Andrew was not aware of these final moments. His face was still hiding, nestled in the elbow of his arm resting on the side of Jesse's bed when, within a matter of seconds, Andrew suddenly sat straight up in his chair, and a swirl of activity began, as an unexpected and magnificent event unfolded, assuring us that not only was Jesse finally free of his precious body, but that the Intelligence which placed us here does not die, it simply changes form.

During those moments I could feel the weight of his spirit as the atmosphere in our private P-ICU room became quite dense. I sensed his spirit was very large and envisioned he would have taken a good deal of pleasure in pushing apart the walls of that room! I looked upward toward the ceiling and all around, and said to him, "Spread out Jesse!" At that moment, to my utter surprise, it was as if Jesse put a feeling inside of me, and in Andrew, too, letting us know without a doubt just how good he felt. It was absolutely astonishing. I began to experience a very odd tickling feeling inside my body that started in my solar plex and spread through my entire body and down through my arms. It was so strong that it made me want to laugh out loud. I could not stop smiling. I was holding back an almost uncontrollable laughter while at the same time feeling completely puzzled by the entire phenomenon. In the midst of these events, Andrew and I looked at each other in sheer amazement. The one thing I was convinced of was that Jesse was doing it! And I could clearly see Andrew was having the same experience when he exclaimed, "He won't let me cry!" I said, "He won't let me cry either!"

Jesse lingered with us for a few minutes this way and then he took his leave into heaven. Nevertheless, I tell you truthfully, I could feel a part of me leave with him, as if a measure of my own life force had literally been drawn away from my body and taken with him. Perhaps it was the part of my life energy that co-mingled with his from the beginning of our lives together. A few short moments afterward I was in a state of shock.

I walked out of the room where he lay throughout the last profound week of our amazing life together, and as I left his beautiful body behind, I began to feel a shroud of darkness blanket me. It permeated my entire being, creating as it were, a thick veil around all I could see, feel, hear, think, or touch, until I found myself sheathed in what resembled the blackest night, and just as vast. It was a feeling beyond description. A paralyzing mix of sorrow and fear consumed me. I was not able to cry. Nor was I fully able to respond to any outer activity for nearly two weeks.

Date: October 4, 2006
To: Group

My precious Jesse David passed away very peacefully in my arms just minutes before 11:00 p.m. last night, Tuesday, October 3, 2006.

A memorial service will be held for Jesse David on Saturday, November 11, 2006, which I will share the details of at a later time.

Sincerely,
Patricia,
Jesse David's Mother

CHAPTER 24

First Light

"Is it really so that the one I love is everywhere?"
~Rumi

ONCE HOME FROM THE HOSPITAL I did not know how I would be able to sleep without Jesse David also with me in the home, much less in this world. My sister Judy, who visited just a few weeks earlier had traveled again from Maryland to assist as much as she was able to throughout Jesse's final week. After a few minutes of conversation, exhausted and solemn, we said good night, and I began a reluctant ascent to my second-story bedroom.

Contemplating the stairs Jesse and I had climbed together so many times before terrified me now. My thoughts raced through my mind. How would I live through this night without him? A paralyzing confusion overwhelmed me with sorrow so profound, and expansive, and demanding, it permeated every nerve and atom of my physical and emotional structure. I reached the top of the stairs where Jesse David's empty room was located to the left, and my own toward the right. I could not look inside his room. I could not bear to not see him there. Confused and weak, and so tragically heartbroken, I made my way to my bed, and looking at the place where Jesse David lay next to me only nights before, I touched the bed as if he were there, wishing I could feel the energy of his life and draw it into my own life. As I lay very still, locked tightly in a fetal position, my heart pounding with fear, I felt a void so great I could not comprehend it. I peered into the darkness, searching the room for some hint of my sanity, and anything that would tell me what to do . . . and where my Jesse David is now. I whispered over and over into the darkness, "I love you Jesse David." Finally, out of sheer exhaustion I closed my eyes, hoping I would find myself with him once more, right where he is, because I could not imagine living one more moment of my life in such a state of sorrow and fear.

And I slept.

> *"They say there is a doorway from heart to heart, but what is the use of a door when there are no walls?"*
> *~Rumi*

A couple hours later, at approximately a quarter past three in the morning, I was stirred awake. I felt an unfamiliar activity around me. As I gained awareness, I discerned a light in the room. It hovered faintly above the end of the bed. I also sensed a vibration of energy. Within moments I realized it was Jesse David. He was checking on me, letting me know he did not leave, assuring me he had only changed form. I was thankful for his closeness to me in the night, because the nighttime was always the most difficult when we both gave so much for him.

After a few minutes of lying awake, feeling his energy throughout the room, I decided to check on my sister, hoping that I would not disturb her. I found her awake, and though I was secretly comforted to not feel so alone in those moments, I apologized for waking her. She told me she was already awake. She said a bright light shone directly on her, waking her from her sleep.

> *"Whoever finds love beneath hurt and grief disappears into emptiness with a thousand new disguises."* ~ *Rumi*

One week after Jesse's transition, at the suggestion of my sister, I took a flight to Maryland to visit with family members who were not able to be with Jesse and me during his final week. I stayed at the home of another sister, Tracey, and her husband, Steven, who live on Maryland's Eastern Shore. Still in a state of shock, I did not cry or give anything more than mere mechanical responses. At the end of my visit I counted two entire weeks lived without Jesse David here, most of which I recall very little of, except the final moments before leaving for the airport to return home.

I walked outside and paced the deck of their house, clutching a warm cup of coffee and staring out at the water ways where Jesse David and I had been a few times during our visits. I remembered us together, gliding around the tributaries near their home in the small pontoon boat my brother-in-law kept docked at the edge of their property. I recalled the picture I took of Jesse sitting next to me in that boat one evening as the sun was setting. Jesse was looking right into the camera's eye, as if he was looking past it and straight into my own eyes.

Jesse David on Uncle Steven's pontoon boat.
Kent Island, Maryland, 2004

As I stood alone in the cool October morning air, seeing the two of us together once more in scenes which now could only be repeated in my memory, I whispered the simplest and yet most profound words I'd spoken since he'd left; "I miss you Jesse David."

I arrived home from Maryland at 11:00 p.m. on a Tuesday night. I sat down at my computer and read through emails and afterward I searched the internet for anything that would occupy my time until I was exhausted enough to go to bed, hoping that by doing so I might be less aware of his presence no longer there. I looked at the time on the computer clock. Three a.m. Still, I was not capable of climbing the stairs to my room. I didn't know how to make myself pass by the empty bedroom that Jesse occupied just three weeks before. I could not bear to look in and not see him there. An hour later, at 4:00 a. m., I was no longer resistant to the weariness of the night and the week away from home. I turned off the computer and as I made my ascent to the second floor, I recalled the few occasions when I didn't understand why Jesse had done something or other, so I would have him write a letter explaining his actions as a way of managing through the issue. He would write his perception of what happened and why, and I would respond with a letter back to him. Afterward, we would talk about the situation. It worked, very well, in fact. And when the issues were put to rest, we loved, trusted, and respected each other even more.

When I reached the top of the stairs, I peered through his opened bedroom door at the empty space. It felt as if I was looking into a void as great as what seemed to be consuming my entire being now. I slowly stepped inside his bedroom, the same timid way I approached my mother the first time I saw her in the hospital. That was over three decades earlier, but this time there was no one to rescue me, there was no one to wrap their arms around me and tell me what to do.

I looked at the place where he used to lay. I looked at his desk, and then at the table next to the couch where he ate his meals and kept his phone and water glass. Nothing felt the same. There was no evidence of the activity I was so fond of, and I could not bear to think of the life that was not with me anymore. I began to cry for the first time since he left. I began searching his room - every corner, nook, and crevice, high and low, hoping to find a letter he may have written to let me know something, anything at all. I found none. And I cried out to God asking Him how much a mother could hurt. I cried until I was exhausted, empty of all my pleas to God and heaven.

Over the next several months the shock did not subside. Instead, it seemed to change form, at times overwhelming my entire existence, like a flood of agonizing sorrow making its way to my conscious heart and mind. Each night I would lie very still, listening to the silence, feeling the pounding of my heart, searching every corner of the darkness for a glimmer of the light that meant my Jesse David was near. I searched all that existed within and around me, and I prayed the Intelligence beating my heart would provide me with some inkling of assurance of my Jesse David's finer existence. And each night, as I closed my eyes to the vast, silent darkness, I would speak out, "I love you Jesse David. I love you very much. I promise I always will. Perhaps you will be near me tonight."

Day and night were no different, except for how I abhorred waking in the morning. It meant I would have to breathe, move, and turn my head to look at things without him there. Even a blank wall was torture to bear. I could hardly swallow, yet I knew I had to eat. I could hardly breathe, yet I forced myself to do it. I forced myself to speak, pretending it was easy when, in fact, I was simply practicing the intonations and expressions I had always used so easily, until now. I tried to hide from others my shattered and terrified reaction to every sight and sound I experienced in the absence of my Jesse David. My very existence was a consuming void so extreme that at times I felt I was in a literal vacuum of space pulling at my very flesh. It felt as if the life within me was not willing to be in this world without the presence of Jesse here also. He had become the reason for my existence, and suddenly my reason and all the activities that characterized it had evaporated in front of my eyes.

I became acutely aware of how, in a flash of moments, everything that defined the last sixteen years of my life had vanished. Nothing was familiar anymore. I did not set alarms through the night, nor did I even want to hear an alarm or look at a clock. I no longer checked on my precious Jesse David or gave him his medications and supplements throughout the day and night. He wasn't there to listen to when he wanted to discuss matters important to him. I no longer had the central point of my life around which my own journey had become accustomed to, and at times the silence was more than I could bear.

It took great determination to rest at night, so I would spend time reading anything I could find that might help me understand what his existence is like now. Upon waking, myriad thoughts and feelings flooded me. I began each day by journaling. Hours upon hours I sat at my computer, typing out impressions which lingered throughout the day and into the evening. My greatest task became piecing together reasons to resume my life in such a way that every moment going forward would honor Jesse. However, this new task was even more difficult than the original, because at least when he was with me, I was able to look upon his face, touch his delicate hand, hold him in my arms, and hear the sound of his precious voice.

In time, as the days and months progressed, I began to find inklings of reasons and motivation in the love that remains and binds us eternally to begin again. Day and night I practiced, aware of each breath I took, enduring every lift of my hand, and facing each turn of my head. Every moment of each new day was carefully calculated, contemplated, and finally achieved, but now I must accomplish it all without the physical presence of my Jesse David as a point of reference, my effortless reason, my greatest motivator.

CHAPTER 25

Remembering Jesse

JESSE DAVID CORNETT
MEMORIAL MESSAGE
November 11, 2006

IN EARLY SEPTEMBER, JESSE WENT INTO the hospital to have a port placed for IV medications, and on one of the quieter afternoons after he was released from ICU to a regular room, I pulled out a book to read to him while he relaxed. And so, he listened as I read The Velveteen Rabbit. When I finished the story, we understood together that toys are not the only things that become real. People become real, and sometimes even children become real. We stayed very quiet in the moments that followed. Perhaps we were simply not able to find the words. Perhaps words were not required. But in his eyes, I could see that we were realizing the same thing; that Jesse David was indeed becoming real. I wrapped my arms around him, held him close for a moment, and said, "I love you Jesse David."

I would like to share with you now about how Jesse David "became real." Though all of it began before he was born, I would like to begin by telling you about his name. It is a very special name. I chose it very carefully. His first name, Jesse, means God Exists. His second name, David, means Beloved. And his last name, Cornett, means Little Crown. And each time I said his name, Jesse David Cornett, I knew I was actually declaring, "God exists, Beloved Little Crown."

Did you ever see my Jesse David? Did you look upon his face? Did you look into his eyes, Golden sunflowers with Green Leaves of Life? Did you look beyond his slender build, the bulge of the G-tube under his shirt, or the lumens that shown beyond his sleeve? Did you talk with him and listen to him speak? Did you hear the wisdom in his youthful voice? Did you listen to him laugh? Did he make you laugh, too?

Did you know my Jesse David, the real Jesse David? If so, you knew a friend for life. Did you teach Jesse David, or counsel Jesse David? If so, you learned many things and gained many insights. When you walked beside my Jesse David, did you slow your pace to keep step with him?

Did you visit my Jesse David? Yes, many of Jesse's friends visited with him. Andrew stayed many long days and nights when Jesse was in the hospital. And others who visited Jesse in our home listened to the motion of equipment through the night. You were awakened by his troubles and you saw his pain, and you returned to him again and again. And to each of you I want to express how much these things meant to Jesse. And for the hope and the strength, and the reason for living you gave to Jesse and for the comfort this gave me, my gratitude shall not cease or even slightly diminish. And it is my prayer that God's compassion follows each of you all the days of your life.

During Jesse's last week among us, many people encouraged me to believe God for the miracle of Jesse's recovery. And I longed for their expectation, but as hope for his recovery dimmed, I began to question within me, "What is a miracle?" Well, as I see it anything God performs, anything at all that God chooses to do *is* a miracle. But, too often we look so hard for our expectation we see right past the thing we hoped for and we end up missing the miracle altogether. But I did not miss the miracle. Not this time, because in my life Jesse David *is* the miracle. And I am so fortunate to have recognized and experienced this amazing truth every day for more than sixteen year.

The very moment I laid eyes on Jesse David, I loved him with all my heart. And understanding my accountability for this precious life trusted to my care God also let me know in His special way He would help me.

As an infant, Jesse was always happy. Throughout his life, Jesse loved laughter and he thrived on laughter. He even laughed out loud before he was even one week old! And in his eyes, behind every glance and every smile, there was always a look of some deeper wisdom that only he beheld. And so perhaps that is why at only two years old, shortly after the earthquake in the summer of 1992 centered near the home we lived in, on a particular day, myself still shaken from the experience, while I held him on my lap reading books to him, Jesse spoke up suddenly and assured me with great confidence, "Jesus is here and He will pick you up!" I was speechless and at the same time comforted. But this would not be the only time that Jesse David would move my heart and my mind between such extremes.

As I watched Jesse grow from infant to a beautiful child, the more I experienced his unique perceptions of his young world the greater was my anticipation to see the *man* Jesse would become. Then on Valentine's Day 1995, I was given the news that Jesse David had Cystic Fibrosis, a life shortening disease. My heart was truly broken on that day. I did not know from where I would find the courage to watch my Jesse David suffer. Nevertheless, I was determined I would not give up trying for him. Even if there seemed to be no hope, I would search for all I could do to help him thrive. And I daily sought God for His help, this promise He gave me before Jesse was born; and for His provision; and for His Wisdom. And not unlike King David in Psalm 139, I prayed, [Lord], "you have searched me, and you know me. You know my sitting down and my rising up. You perceive my thoughts from afar. You search out my path and my lying down, and are acquainted with all my ways. For there is not a word on my tongue, but behold, [O Lord] you know it altogether. You hem me in behind and before. You laid your hand on me. This knowledge is beyond me. [It is] lofty. I [cannot] attain it." (W.E.B,

Psalm 139, verses 1 – 6)

I asked God to watch over us. For "where could I go from your Spirit? Or where could I flee from your [Love]? If I ascend up into heaven, you are there. If I make my bed in Sheol, behold, you are there! If I take the wings of the [morning], and settle in the uttermost parts of the sea, even there your hand will lead me, and your right hand will hold me." (W.E.B, Psalm 139, verses 7 – 10)

I asked for wisdom and for courage. "If I say, "Surely the darkness will overwhelm me. The light around me will be night," even the darkness doesn't hide from you, but the night shines as the day. The darkness is like light to you." (W.E.B, Psalm 139, verses 11 – 12)

And continually I asked God to strengthen Jesse's body. "For you formed [his] inmost being. You knit [him]together in [his] mother's womb. I will give thanks to you, for [he is] fearfully and wonderfully made. Your works are wonderful. My soul knows that very well. [His] frame wasn't hidden from you, when [he] was made in secret, woven together in the depths of the earth. Your eyes saw [his] body. In your book they were all written, the days that were ordained for [him], when as yet there were none of them." (W.E.B, Psalm 139, verses 13 – 16)

And although I often struggled in the depths of my soul, I believed God would perfect that which concerns us in this earthly journey and for eternity. "How precious to me are your thoughts, God! How vast is their sum! If I would count them, they are more in number than the sand. When I wake up, I am still with you." (W.E.B, Psalm 139, verses 17 – 18) "Search me, O God, and know my heart. Try me and know my thoughts. See if there is any [grievous] way in me and lead me in the way everlasting." (W.E.B, Psalm 139, verses 23 – 24)

Throughout Jesse's last week among us I desired in the time

I had left with him to absorb all I could of his amazing life. I contemplated this beautiful soul I love so deeply, eternally, who had indeed suffered, and tragically so, for too long inside his delicate, young body. Truly, I found it difficult to understand why this tender life would be cut so short. Why was it, that even the short time given us should have been consumed with such suffering as he endured? However, even while these questions stirred deep within me, I felt a peace within me that caused me to believe there must be a greater plan, one that I cannot fathom; a plan worthy of these things; a plan worthy of the life Jesse David lived. I began to believe there must be a plan for Jesse David's life perfectly conceived to fit into an amazing Master design, intricately woven of *every* life. And so, I trust my questions and my longing for Jesse in time will be quieted within me.

Time was a precious commodity which Jesse, recognized well from his youth. He did not want to miss one day or even one moment of his life. Neither did I, and even more now in his final days.

Now one of the many important things that characterized the time Jesse and I spent together was the way we talked about everything, even from his earliest years.

"Do worms have chins?" "No." I explained. "They'd trip on them." "You know, Mom, there *is* such a thing as a family of Birds." And I said, "Jesse David, you are *my* family." "There's a boy at school who's mean to me." "Well, maybe he wants to be your friend and doesn't know how to get your attention."

"Tell me your thoughts, Mom, of God and Jesus and Heaven?" "Your name means God exists, my Beloved Jesse David."

"I wish blood could be tested without being stuck with a needle." "I want to be a herpetologist, because I think it's possible reptiles hold cures for diseases." "Here is my plan for perpetual energy." And I would always reply, "You know, Jesse David, great things are waiting to be done by you."

"Well, Mom the way I see it, with a transplant I only have

finites to consider". And revealing the palms of his hands, first the left then the right, he continued, "Either I will die on the table or I will live five years." And carefully I listened, and I watched him, feeling the extremes once again, both amazed and heart broken in the very same moment. For there was my Jesse David balancing his very own life in his delicate young hands.

Jesse loved knowledge. He would read entire sets of encyclopedias for pleasure and did so at least three times over. And when Jesse was in tenth grade, he explained to me that he had to learn the really big things first, because if he spent time on the little things, he may not have time to learn the most important things. And so, it came as no surprise when he came home from school one day with a book on Quantum Physics tucked under his arm. He was going to learn this on his own.

Jesse thrived on the company and conversation of others. Whether young, or old, or peers, people were drawn to him. Fascinated by him, people would seek him out. But do we need to wonder why? For knowing Jesse David, whether up close and personal, or from afar, one simply could not have experienced him without being affected in some positive way. You see, Jesse understood and respected the importance of dignity for himself and others. He fully acknowledged and willingly embraced others' right to individuality. And Jesse possessed the unique ability to assure others of their worth in his own skillful and transparent manner. And as I recounted the manner in which this beautiful young soul lived the few years given him, I considered the strengths he possessed in his character.

Jesse David was imaginative. He was assertive, yet considerate. He was patient, kind, and compassionate. And even on those occasions when things seemed to go terribly wrong for Jesse, his actions were not void of reason and I learned to trust his methods for their inherent wisdom.

Jesse's outlook was always positive. He preferred activities that indicated a normalcy to his life. In fact, the times that I told him how sorry I was for all he must endure, Jesse would always reply, "It's okay, Mom. Many others have it much worse than I do."

And so gathering within me the sum of Jesse David, the character that defined him, and all that he'd become, I realized that right in front of me, so peacefully, so quietly, right where he lay, within my reach and yet so far away from me, I *was* beholding *the man*. And again, I was comforted, and I was humbled, because I was not deprived of this desire that I had so greatly anticipated. For certainly Jesse David had indeed become a man while yet in his youth. And I believe one way we can keep Jesse David close to our hearts is by also taking on more of these qualities in our own lives, these priceless gifts he showed to us and live them toward others throughout our life.

In Jesse's final hour, while holding him in my arms, this heart of mine living outside my body, so beautiful before my eyes, as he performed his final task so skillfully and gracefully, I loved him more deeply than ever.

Now, my life has been so very blessed by Jesse David. What a great privilege that Jesse David and his Birth Mother, and most of all God trusted me to love and care for Jesse. I am so fortunate, because I was the one chosen to be Jesse's mother; chosen to experience the miracle of Jesse David every day and every hour of his precious life; a miracle more evident, ever lovelier, and more mysterious, even as his life grew more difficult for him to bear. And as all who allowed Jesse David to touch their life, the gift and privilege of Jesse David in my life has changed me into someone I never knew I would be.

A couple months ago, one of the most courageous conversations Jesse and I encountered took place in a hotel room where we stayed on a particular evening as we managed through his transplant evaluations. We talked together quietly, intelligently and lovingly of what the future might hold for him. And making our way through that awesome, yet tragic conversation, forcing silent and staying still my shredded heart feeling so completely overwhelmed within me, I listened carefully as Jesse lay out before me exactly what he desired for his final hours. And Jesse asked that whenever I think of him, that I always "remember how close we are." Now, I did not take these things lightly, because to fulfill his request precisely as he intended, I am required to understand exactly what *he* meant. So, I went back to the start of us, the foundation that held us so securely. "Sewn together at the hip" is how I have often described us. But we are closer than that, because it was inside my heart that Jesse was formed before he was born. And closer still are we, because we are bonded as mother and child, mysteriously, eternally, through a loving plan of God.

And now I am not the same because of the gift, the miracle, this amazing Love that changed me, My Precious Jesse David. And so, with all my heart and ten thousand times, I must say again, I love you Jesse David. I always will.

Love,
Mom

Mom and Jesse David, age 15.5
November 5, 2005
By permission of Turville Photography,
Orange, California

CHAPTER 26

Silence Is Golden

WHEN I ARRIVED HOME FROM THE memorial service I could see as I stepped out of the car it had rained ever so lightly. I made my way inside the house and a few minutes later the neighbor's dog began to cry out in such a way that the sound reverberated throughout the entire neighborhood, breaking the silence pervading my very existence. And it cried that same eerie way for several evenings after. I had never heard such a sound. It seemed odd to me; the rain that fell only in the area around our home, mixed with the spellbinding sound of such deep mourning, and yet these things were also strangely comforting. I wondered if everything in all of nature sensed Jesse David was gone from this world. It was as if they were mourning with me, and for me; helping me, because I could not express the profoundness of it all, at least not the way I felt it.

It is said that Silence is golden. I've often contemplated the deeper meaning of that cliché. I have learned to love the silence, and so perhaps it is no wonder I am fascinated by the inherent qualities of silence. I have come to believe the silence holds secrets it would easily reveal if we would simply stop the clamoring of our own thoughts, shut out the inner noise, and listen for what the quietude is trying to express to us. Silence, wherein does reside the beginning of all creation, is a substrate for opportunities to contemplate, review, imagine, and expand our creativity, as well as draw into our intellect and our understanding things yet unrealized. By quieting the inner response, we are able to harmonize our feelings and align our expectations. In so doing, we open ourselves to the eventual transmutation of frustration or disappointment, and this is one of the most liberating acts we can embrace. Silence is a doorway to the peace, the illumination, and the adjustment of all conditions, and we can send forth this control to harmonize activities even before we ever enter them. Once we understand the proper use of every supply afforded us, and as our activity gains momentum, even more of Life's secrets will be revealed.

THE SUPPLY OF FRIENDSHIP

Many of Jesse David's friends stayed close to me during the three months I remained in California after Jesse's transition. I recall the feeling of awe that struck me when, just a couple days after Jesse passed, I received a call from Chris who stayed with Jesse at our home much of the time during the summer months when school was out. He and two others who also knew Jesse wanted to visit with me. When they arrived, I sat with them in conversation, feeling a deep longing to hear anything they had to express. And when I asked them if Jesse knew how much I loved him, they enthusiastically assured me that he did know. "Oh, yes!" they said. "You were the best mother a kid could have!" Then they asked if they could go up to Jesse's bedroom, the way they used to. It was such a comfort to me that helped ease the void I felt. And Andrew, who was with Jesse David in his last hour, stayed with me day and night for almost two months. These and many other important and tenderhearted friends of Jesse visited often.

One afternoon after Andrew was out of school for the day

we went to the mall where he and Jesse used to meet up. Andrew and I had lunch at the food court and afterward we decided to walk along the shops where Jesse David and I had also walked together on many occasions, retracing the steps we had taken with Jesse before. As we entered the mall from the food court, we were fascinated at a butterfly that somehow found its way inside the building. It fluttered around Andrew and then managed to find his right shoulder where it landed quite naturally and stayed for several minutes. To Andrew and me there was no question whatsoever that Jesse David was letting him know how much he loves him still, we were certain of it! What we were not sure of was how long Andrew would carry the butterfly on his shoulder, just as he carried Jesse David so lovingly in his heart.

Other friends of Jesse visited on many occasions. Shelley, Matt, and Chris, accompanied by others, some who I was meeting for the first time, but who knew Jesse well, came and went freely. They often stayed for hours, and sometimes days at a time. The girls would spend time watching movies and talking girl-talk, and the boys spent most of their time relaxing in Jesse's room, just as they had done whenever they visited Jesse.

Jesse's two older birth brothers, also stayed with me from the time they arrived for the memorial service, until Thanksgiving Day when I drove them home to Visalia where I spent two days with Jesse's entire birth family. While they were with me, they cooked meals, we shared our enjoyment of music and their passion for art which they practiced with the advantage of Jesse's computer. Had these bold and loving young friends not needed the comfort of Jesse's presence once more, as did I, I may not have survived emotionally.

Although I felt a profound sorrow and confusion, I was still able to perceive Jesse's love alive, active, and very interested in my well-being. It was a great challenge for me to eat, or even go into the kitchen where I had prepared so many things for him; supplements and medications, as well as meals we both hoped he would be able to eat – and keep down. One afternoon I noticed light in the shape of a person about Jesse's size appear in the dining room near the dining table. I watched, completely fixated, unsure of what caused it, as it glided across the dining room wall and then wrapping around the corner leading into the kitchen. It moved through the doorway into the kitchen where it hovered on the front of the refrigerator. I considered whether I had created it somehow. Was it a reflection? Was I having a hysterical response to missing Jesse? I moved about the room, opening and closing doors several times, and tried to think of every physical possibility for what might have caused the phenomenon. I was never able to replicate the activity. Nor could I explain how the light moved in such a way as to turn around corners of the walls. I wondered if Jesse David was coaxing me into the kitchen, encouraging me to eat. Eating was his greatest struggle during his final months, and now it was mine as well. Unsure of anything, I realized I must do my best in all things, because Jesse also did his best.

A WALK IN THE PARK

In early November Jesse's cousin, Carli, invited me to join her on a visit to the Huntington Library Museum to tour the gardens surrounding it. There were many different garden settings such as a Zen garden, an English garden, a desert garden, a rose garden, and many other themes. I believe Carli's favorite was the Zen garden. She sat inside its boundaries on a bench and became very still for a few moments. I watched as she seemed to be meditating, or perhaps she was simply drawing in its qualities. I did not ask. I simply let that be her private enjoyment. We noticed everything as we walked the paths perfectly lined and creatively trimmed in all sorts of trees, shrubs, and foliage. As the sun began to set, taking with it the warmth it provided throughout the day, we made our way to the museum gift shop to browse for mementos and remembrances of our visit before leaving.

At the end of a very special day I was glad to be home. I felt closer to Jesse surrounded by the things that were familiar to our life. I sat very still on the couch in the living room thinking about him for a few moments. I wondered if he was aware of my love for him, and if he knew how I had spent the day. As I reached for the bag from the museum gift shop next to me, I recalled the items I purchased; two note cards and a music cd – the peaceful music I often keep playing softly in the background. But to my surprise, I found something I did not expect; a third note card. It had a picture of a dragonfly on it. It was beautiful, but I was startled to find it in the bag, certain I did not pay for it, because I didn't pick it out, though I likely would have if I had even noticed it among the cards I browsed. I looked at the receipt and was glad to see the cashier had charged me for it. Nevertheless, I could not figure out how I ended up with it. I remembered the dragonfly that landed on Jesse that peaceful day in August. Was he using this dragonfly as a symbol of the peace he wanted me to find?

CHAPTER 27

The Agreement

"Wanting to know reasons, knocking on a door. It opens. I've been knocking from the inside." ~ Rumi

I BELIEVE GOD SPEAKS TO EACH of us in ways that reach the individual on terms they can connect with. God is not haphazard, nor is the plan for each life. Yes, God helped me. Although my desire was for Jesse to have a healthy, happy life, I realize now that there are often activities unfolding a purpose greater than I may recognize at any given time. Even experiencing the profound love that we shared, what was not clear to me throughout Jesse's life here is that he was working out an agreement he made before he ever entered this life, as with me, and I believe it is true for each of us.

December 22nd movers took most everything from our home in preparation for my move back to Maryland. I spent the evening in that silent, empty space, now void of the only tangible reminders I had left of what defined my life only a matter of weeks before. I set about packing a few stray items into boxes that I planned to ship to myself, thinking they would be delivered at the same time I arrived in Maryland. As I sorted through what remained, an intense surge of memories began to overwhelm my thoughts and feelings.

I had never stopped wondering if there was something else of significance I could have done for Jesse while caring for his life; something that would have made a difference in the quality, strength, and longevity he so much deserved. As that question flooded my mind now, intermingled with the memories I combed through in what seemed to be seconds flashing by, a severe panic came over me. In my mind I sifted through each attempt and every method I had employed to help Jesse thrive, at the same time afraid of recognizing anything I may have missed. The panic mounted, and just when it seemed the onslaught of thoughts was going to take me completely down, I picked up a book I had abandoned half way through reading it months before that was lying among the items scattered around me on the floor that remained to be packed. I frantically began to flip through the pages at the back of the book that I hadn't had the chance to read. I wasn't actually searching for anything specific. I was simply doing anything I could think of to make the panic subside when I came upon a list of positive thoughts and quotes. As I read each one, I could feel the shift within me from despair to awe as I began to realize I *had* done everything I knew to do for Jesse – at the time. But more than that, I would have done anything I could have. Then, I began to recognize the amazing and powerful agreement Jesse David had worked out for his own life. I sensed the sacredness of that agreement was not to be argued with. It was between Jesse David and God. Perhaps I was simply a facilitator as he accomplished the plan laid out for his life. I wanted a child to love, and he and God responded. Was this enough? Was it all the comfort I longed for? No. It never is. Like a rose bud tightly bound, seemingly dormant awaiting the time of its awakening, nothing is ever enough, until I see him face to face once more. Nevertheless, it provided a perspective that helped me understand how my role in Jesse's life was also, in essence, my own agreement between God and me.

I arrived in Maryland December 29, 2006 and a month later

I took a trip to South Africa to personally meet and visit with the young man who was the first to use the inhaled L-Arginine and Glutathione regimen that is the subject of the hypothesis paper I completed the year before. When I returned home on February 5th, the first snow of the season covered the ground with a fine, sparkling white layer that was new to my eyes once more after having lived for twenty-six years in Southern California.

I was still not working, and for the time being that was good for me. During the months that followed I continued reading and journaling my thoughts and feelings each day. One morning in early February 2007, upon waking at 6:00 a. m. I hurriedly made my way to the bedroom I'd set up as my office space. I turned on the computer and quickly began typing out all the thoughts and revelations that flooded my heart and mind before it all faded into my longing for Jesse David near me once more.

> *All your attempts to reach me are in reality my attempts*
> *to reach you." ~ Rumi*

I hardly noticed the hours that had passed; that is until the landline phone rang. I looked at the clock next to the handset on the table across the room. The red lighted numbers shown 10:10 a. m., and since it was a weekday, I was certain no one I knew would be calling. Everyone was at work. I looked at the caller ID expecting to see a solicitor's number, or an untraceable incoming call. However, as I focused in on the display, I was surprised to see my own name. I wasn't sure if I should pick up or see how long it would go on ringing, since there was no way I knew of that the call could have originated from my own landline! I was completely perplexed by it. As kids, my siblings and I used to play silly games on the phone, dialing random numbers, and telling harmless jokes about refrigerators running fast, or eggs being too fresh. On more than one occasion, out of curiosity, I dialed our own home phone number. I was never surprised when I got a busy signal. That made sense; the line is in use. What didn't make sense this time, however, was how my phone generated a call on its own – to itself?

In those fleeting moments, my heart pounding and hands shaking, I picked up the handset not certain if that would end the call or if I would simply hear the drawn-out beeping sound of a busy signal. However, neither is what happened. Instead, the line was open. I listened to the dim sounds of electrical pulses coming from what seemed to be nowhere and everywhere at the same time. Not certain what to make of it all, I said "Hello", but to whom I wasn't sure. I listened, and there was only more of the vast, open silence, softly emitting the pulses of energy. I said "Hello" again, but there was only silence in reply. So, I spoke once more, this time telling Jesse David that I love him with all my heart. I listened for a few moments to the silence, and to my own thoughts spinning, before I was able to hang up the call, letting go of the experience, feeling as though I was letting go of Jesse David once more. "Bye, bye my Precious. I love you very much"

One of the most common occurrences that continued for over two years was the constant need to replace light bulbs. Two years into this phenomenon I began saving the bulbs I replaced, just to get an idea of how many I went through in an average month. In the beginning, right after Jesse's transition, it was one or two each day. Two years later, it was only two or three times a month. And more than once, even as I was still turning the new light bulb into the socket, I watched as a grey mist curled around clouding the globe and consuming all the visible space inside until it was no longer clear. The new light bulb was ruined before it had even been fully placed in the light fixture.

Another consistent pattern that lasted for at least two years was the malfunction of electronic devices that rely on light, such as CD and DVD players. They regularly skipped or stopped altogether. At first, I had no clue what was going on. I wondered how every electronic device I owned could have been faulty. I gave away devices that I believed were not working properly, only to learn that they worked fine for the person who took them. Once I made the connection that all the devices use light, I understood how to work around it. I started using low wattage CFL light bulbs in the home, and I closed the doors of the entertainment amour where the CD and DVD units were housed to diminish the interference. However, the CD player in the car still skipped and I had little recourse but to eject and reinsert the disk.

Often this type of activity is attributed to the presence of our loved ones who have left this world, which certainly may be the case at times, although I believe the phenomena is also due to the extremely high vibrational uptick in the emotional and physical body of those who remain. As our own physical structure adjusts to the increased vibrational rate, such occurrences will diminish. That does not mean, however, that our loved ones are no longer near at times, or that they have lost interest in us. Love is an Eternal flame, a bond that will not be breached, and cannot fail.

Approaching Jesse's 17th birthday, my plan was to manage peacefully throughout the day, and that evening two of my sisters would join me to honor Jesse's birthday. But when I arose in the morning, I was not in the emotional state I envisioned I would be. Still, I was determined to go through the motions. After showering I stood in front of the bathroom mirror working to steady my hand while stepping through my usual ritual of make-up and hair. Within moments, one of the large decorative light bulbs above the mirror shattered for no reason I could detect, spraying shards of glass all over the counter, sink, and floor. That only added to my trembling state of being. I cleaned up the glass and hoped there would not be a repeat before I was finished grooming myself.

Afterward, with little to tend to throughout the day, I sat and waited for the hours to pass. My thoughts raced relentlessly at a debilitating speed. I couldn't separate any one of them well enough to work through them. I couldn't cry. I couldn't even move. The only thing I could perceive was the chasm that separated us, and for hours I gasped shallow breaths that began to take on the rhythm of the ventilator in Jesse's hospital room during his final week. Exhausted at day's end, I was grateful for the sleep that seized my consciousness during the night.

April 2007, I began seeking employment. I knew it was time to bring a familiar routine back into my life. One month later I accepted a contract position with an IT firm, and in mid-June I made good on a promise to come back to California to visit Jesse's friends for a couple days. After two days in Orange County, I spent the remainder of the trip in San Diego to reunite with two friends I met when I traveled to South Africa. They had been profoundly supportive of me across the miles.

Throughout September I wasn't sure how well I would navigate the first anniversary of Jesse's leaving. I stepped carefully through each day, incorporating simple gestures that occupied the time, when before I would otherwise have been checking on him, bringing him a meal, giving him a supplement or a medication, or just looking in to say, "I love you". I had already replaced many of those activities with other rituals. I realized that tea lights kept a soft glow flickering around the home and lasted about the same number of hours as the intervals between Jesse's supplement regimen. And I often whispered my words of love to Jesse in heaven, all the while hoping he would let me know he was not far away.

One evening, while relaxing on my balcony, feeling the warm, calm weather of an Indian summer, I noticed a dragonfly at the sliding door next to where I sat. It was working with great determination to get inside. I remembered the dragonfly that landed on Jesse David a year before. Feeling the memory as real as the original experience, I opened the sliding door, and it easily found its way inside. Then, I realized it would die if it stayed inside, so I tried to figure out how to get it back outside. I was afraid to pick it up, so I asked Jesse what I should do, and in the very same breath I remembered Jesse was also afraid of the dragonfly that landed on him, but he stayed still at my request. I knew then exactly what I must do, and I tried to be brave. I wondered if dragonflies really do give us energy. As I maneuvered it onto my hand, I stayed very steady, and I could feel its wings vibrating, though I could not see them moving. I walked out to the balcony and sat in a chair, my attention fixed on the vibration moving through my hand and up into my forearm. It was the most fascinating feeling; like a tickle.

As it turned out I managed quite peacefully through that first anniversary, relatively speaking.

CHAPTER 28

Surrender

I HAVE BECOME AWARE OF THE power that exists within and without; the innate wisdom that guides us into and through experiences purposed for the perfecting of our soul. The Divine Source of our existence is the very energy that animates our physical structure, beats our heart, and illumines the intellect, and if we utilize the laws and energy of Life consciously and constructively, with strictly pure motives, we will reap that which is ultimately a perfecting result. To do otherwise will only serve to complicate the lesson, adding layers that must eventually be stripped away before the original lesson can be learned.

Aside from the sometimes-unexpected enlightenments we each experience, learning the most profound lessons is not usually accomplished without a perceived sacrifice for which we may search out every manner of avoidance, because we abhor the idea of loss and pain. Avoidance is our response to the fear of experiencing loss, and although we gladly embrace the revelations and greater freedom that always result from lessons accomplished, we would prefer to gain this outcome by our own intellectually devised, painless, or even magically infused method. Fortunately, or perhaps not, our humanly devised methods never accomplish the task of teaching us the lessons that are meant to perfect us, because we simply cannot discern by our human intellect what is necessary to create a permanent and balanced healing of our heart and soul.

I am learning that the innate wisdom within us, by way of its direct connection to the perfect, intelligent, all-loving Source of life, is able to adjust circumstances and lead us to a perfect outcome, because this Wisdom is functioning in the realm of Perfection. When we become aware of this truth and recognize the diversions the human intellect creates as avoidance measures, we are much more likely to surrender to the work of the Divine.

It is also important to embrace a compassionate attitude toward one's self, forgiving as we progress through the healing process, continually invoking Forgiveness. We must learn to draw into our very existence the force of the Divine Love that consumes and transmutes fear, perceptions of loss, feelings of sorrow and anger over what we believe a given outcome should have been. And as we practice letting go of the *fear* of loss, we more fully recognize and willingly embrace the tremendous Love guiding us in perfect wisdom.

One of the most wonderful enlightenments (another word for miracle) anyone can experience is to finally recognize our Teachers in life. These actors, some invited and others who intrude, who come and sometimes go, in and out of the scenes of our life through the various curtains (veils) we draw about us often do not themselves realize the significance of their own role in another's life, or of another's role in their own life. Seldom do we realize the experiences we construct, or draw into our life, are lessons intended to teach our self the very love and forgiveness necessary to transcend conditions. These conditions are simply substrates of activity – a means to an end – like a road that leads to another road on a self-propelled journey where we finally achieve the mastery we seek.

To be a Master simply do as the Masters do. It all comes down to Love, from a motive of Love. And if it is not possible to exercise (Divine) Love under a given set of circumstances in order to Master a condition, then we can always go quietly into our own heart and draw forth Compassion, and then invoke the Forgiveness which adjusts all things, and heals all things, beginning with our own heart.

CHAPTER 29

Poems, Prayers and Promises

LOVE

Why is it so hard to tell her how I feel?
It should be easy, but I can't bring myself to do it.
It's not the same with you; it's not like the other girls.
It's a different feeling, a feeling of constant wonder.
Do I look okay?
Will I see her today?
What will she say to me?
It's a terrible, wonderful thing that I can't get rid of.
But I don't want to get rid of it.
It makes me mourn and dance with glee.
It's a feeling of want, need;
An indescribable feeling of pleasure,
And pain.

Jesse David Cornett
3/2005

LETTER TO JESSE

"And in the sweetness of friendship let there be laughter,
and sharing of pleasures." ~ Kahlil Gibran

March 2013
Dear Jesse,

SIX YEARS IS A LONG TIME to miss someone. Nevertheless, here I am, six years later still missing you. I miss your voice - both of them. I miss the voice I would hear at school: eager and energetic. Then there is the voice I would hear late at night on the phone: calm, confident and carefree. That's the one I miss the most. I miss walking around school with you before first period, making our way to the gym to sit on the rail and talk some more. Those were the times that high school wasn't such a burden.

Do you know what else I really miss? How smart you were. You just got things. You understood such complex theories and you were able to explain them to others in such a way that they didn't seem so complex. You were brilliant; so much more than any of our teachers, and they knew it too. I loved watching you debate with them, but the best was when you would correct them. You were so polite about it; polite but confident. I would just sit next to you, beaming, so proud to call you my friend.

We didn't have long together, but in the few years we did have, you gave me enough friendship, kindness and laughs to sustain me for my lifetime.

Please keep watching over us. Keep showing yourself to me in all the little ways. And make sure when it's my time for Heaven that yours is the first face I see.

Love,
Shelley

MY FACE

Eyes: Golden Sunflowers
With green leaves of life.

Hair: A wave of the warm Caribbean Sea,
Gently crashing against a sand-colored forehead.

Cheeks: Plump and slender all at once;
Like a palm tree in the sun.

Nose: Petite, like a pebble,
Shaped by the sea and faded by the sun.

Jesse Cornett
2005

LETTER FROM SHELLEY
March 2013

*"When you are sorrowful look again in your heart, and
you shall see that in truth you are weeping for that which
has been your delight." ~ Kahlil Gibran*

I've cried since he has been gone because I never told him
how I felt about him. I loved him then and I love him still. I've
cried because I should have said goodbye. I should have touched
his hand or said something out loud to fill the space between us in
those moments. I've cried because I should have stayed. I've cried
because I never got the chance to go back. I just cried.

Jesse was a beautiful, intelligent, inquisitive, sensitive, warm,
loving, strong man. And I cannot thank you enough for raising
your son to be who he was, because who he has changed who I
am forever. You are incredible. I love you so much.

I've struggled in my mind over why I didn't cherish time with
him more. He was terminal; we all knew it. I knew it; I knew our
time was limited, so why couldn't I treat every day with that in
mind? Finally, I understand, and it is so simple. I just did not look
at him and see 'sick'. He was so insecure about his weight and the
G-tube, but I never saw those things. I didn't see a weak body. I
saw the strongest spirit I have ever known. CF did not define him
in my mind. In fact, my family was surprised to learn he had CF,
because I never told them. Why would I? That's not what he was.
He was smart, and funny, honest, and kind, handsome, and gentle.
Not sick. Not dying. Not to me. To me he was invincible. And I
am thankful I saw him that way. If I had treated him as if he was
made of porcelain that could break too easily, how would he have
felt? He knew his diagnosis; he didn't need to see it every day in my
eyes. I just hope that what he did see reflecting back at him through
me was how incredible he was. I hope he noticed how I would
light up when I saw him, and how no one else mattered when he

was standing in front of me. So yes, in the deepest part of my core I knew he was struggling, but his spirit was so strong he outshone CF.

At school a certain girl in our biology class was often unkind toward Jesse. He would cough a lot in class, and she would turn around with a disgusted look on her face and tell him to stop. Then, one time when she did that, he very calmly and with a smile on his face, told her he couldn't help it. He then explained (to the entire class at this point) what CF is and how it was affecting him and why he coughed. After that, she never said a thing to him about again.

Patricia Cornett

DETERMINED

People ask me so many questions.
Some I have no answers to.
Well I'm proud to be special,
Proud to be skinny; proud to cough.
I'm a Cystic Fibrosis patient,
Determined to live.
CF patient, that's me.

People make assumptions:
"You're weak"; "You're not strong".
Well I'm weak in arm, but not in heart.
I'm a CF patient,
Determined to live.
Determined CF patient;
That's me.

Jesse Cornett
2005

PSALM FOR JESSE
Author, Andrew Cadogan

I see Jesse alive in your words. Jesse was so bright it burned. I certainly loved him. In fact, my interest in him was incessant, and that confused me.

I recall the time early in our friendship when I erred toward him, yet, without any condemnation whatsoever he corrected me. He never held it against me; he forgave me, and in the same moment fixed the problem. Through that event Jesse showed his higher understanding, and as a result I was no longer confused.

Not only was he wise, Jesse would bring insight to others as well. His presence was a force, like a magnet. Once grounded in it, you just circled around him, as if in orbit. It felt timeless, and I never even stopped to think when it would end.

CHAPTER 30

The Reassurance

IT SEEMS THAT JESSE KNEW ME very well. He knew I am an analytical thinker and I don't care for clichés. In fact, I have unstrung riddles my entire life trying to answer my own questions of life – my life – in a way that settles a given issue once and for all.

December 22, 2006, while the movers were busy loading my belongings on a truck in preparation for my move from California, I spoke about Jesse with the supervisor who was overseeing the move effort. He revealed to me that while working in Jesse's bedroom, he could feel the energy of Jesse's immense suffering in his own body. In fact, I saw him when I peeked into the room at one point tapping on his chest, and I could see he was feeling some sort of discomfort. I thought perhaps he had a muscle spasm. He encouraged me by saying that Jesse wants me to know he is going to stay close to me until I *get better*. That puzzled me, because I wasn't sick, so I believed the gentleman meant, until I *feel* better. I interpreted his message as a kind attempt to impart some comfort, but it sounded too much like a cliché. I thanked him and wrote it off as insignificant.

Two years later, while visiting with a friend, she expressed the exact words I had heard two years before; "He wants you to know he is going to stay close to you until you *get better*." Well, now he has my attention. How could two people three thousand miles apart who never knew him and did not know each other, express the exact same words; a statement that now seemed more like a riddle than a cliché. And for the next two days I pondered the message, wondering what he meant by *"until I get better."* I turned the words over in my mind repeatedly, and when the phrase *"get better"* started to seem familiar, I believed I had simply been thinking about it too much. Then it was as if I could hear the words, like the foggy memory of a dream.

Finally, like a rush of wind I was there again, standing bedside in his hospital room, reliving my last question to him, "Jesse, do you want to get better?" I recalled how he raised his eyebrows very high, and I remembered thinking that we both knew he would not come out of that crisis. In those moments it all made perfect sense! His answer was, in fact, yes. He wanted to get better, but he meant the ultimate yes, the perfect healing. He raised his eyebrows as high as he could because he wanted Heaven. And this message he spent two years trying to get through to me was to let me know he is staying close to me until I also "get better" – until I also get to Heaven.

When I prayed God would allow me to be a mother, when I asked God if my son could be born in March, I also told God I would never doubt His existence again. We do that, you know. We have no doubt God exists when our experiences are all that we hope for. And we question God's existence – if we aren't blaming him – when circumstances cause us disappointment, sorrow, grief, or fear. I certainly had wavered in my faith many times up to that point throughout my life. But this answer, this gift, would be a permanent, never-ending reminder that God's activity in my life cannot be denied. And like a conversation with the one He has created, an arrangement was unfolded that would accomplish our agreement, and I can think of no aspect of my desire, prayed and then quietly trusted, that was not addressed with precision detail.

Life will always lead us to a greater freedom, creating a

foundation that gives us the courage to continue accomplishing our own agreements. This very activity has been an increasing strength and beauty in my life, even as I remain ever mindful that I *will* see him once more, face to face, never again to know any separation between us.

CHAPTER 31

Don't Miss the Miracle

I BELIEVE THE BIBLICAL STORY OF the talents is not merely a financial exercise, but also presents a lesson regarding every particle of Life's energy poured into us each moment, from the very breaths we breathe, to the beating of our heart, from the thoughts we think, to all we ever intend and succeed at doing. God's Presence is in this physical world by virtue of His Life expressing through each one of us. And I believe the purpose of placing this magnificent Presence of Life here is so that conditions in this physical realm can be raised into a greater and greater perfection. We are the ones who are responsible for raising all Life out of suffering. We are not free until every individual is free, and every moment of our existence is an opportunity to free our self and others. Every moment is an opportunity to draw into our thoughts and feelings the mind of Christ, whereby we are using the Mind of Perfection, and then sending this same activity out to every person, place, condition, and experience we encounter, as well as what we do not encounter. And as the momentum of the greater perfection increases, more of the heavenly activities will be drawn into this world. This activity is the mechanism by which we are able to raise life, and even the earth itself, into the new heaven and the new Earth.

As I've made my way through each new day since Jesse's

transition, I have searched for what I am to do while I remain, and what should be my motive. I've realized the most effective way to manage every aspect of my life begins with keeping my feelings harmonized, and caring for my life the same way I cared for Jesse, with all the same determination, compassion, commitment, and love, so that I can become the higher activities and ever-increasing perfection of Life, as well as a channel for those activities to flow out to others.

We are each uniquely individualized expressions of God's Love – the Energy of Life manifest in this world. No one else will love the way you do, smile the way you do, or see the stars or the trees the way you do. No one else will experience the world the way you will. And no one else will respond to the magnificent power and beauty of Life the way you will. No one else can do what you do quite the way you do it. So, with each step you take, through every experience you face, no matter where your journey leads, don't miss the miracle of you!

CHAPTER 32

Rain Dance

"If in the twilight of memory, we should meet once more,
we shall speak again together, and you shall sing to me
a deeper song." ~ Kahlil Gibran

IT IS A RAINY SATURDAY MORNING, April 11, 2009. I am preparing
to move again. I have moved a thousand times in my life, never
really feeling I have found home. The only resemblance of home
I ever felt was wherever Jesse David and I were together.

I'm listening to Yanni, the music Jesse requested the last night
that we spent together in our home. I could not find the CD, so
I offered him something similarly melodic called *Heavenly*. He
put his headset on and rested to the music flowing into his mind.

Now I listen to the very music I wish I could have provided
at his precious request. *In the Mirror* plays. I've always felt that song
conveys the melody of my soul. Indeed, if it were the only song
in the entire universe, I would not tire of it.

Watching the rain, each drop rides its airy journey, coursing
a path in rhythm and time, like a Rain Dance, and I wonder
just how many there are. More than the stars I search in every
clear night sky, and as I do, I whisper "I love you" into that vast
Consciousness that holds my heart a willing captive?

Perhaps the music has made an agreement with the rain; each

note a generous, compassionate, willing assist; an accompaniment to those drops falling in search of their final, silent, resting place. Do they fall in anticipation of their tranquility in an achievement that cannot be undone? Is there such a harmonious agreement between them that singly, or many at once, the drops fall again and again in perfect time, as if at the exact moment they meld as one with their final destination they ignite each note of the melody, sometimes slowly, sometimes sweeping, sometimes full, and sometimes resting?

And as I consider this beauty of nature and song, I think of the greatest love I have known in this earthly life; a love that I am sure has been from the very beginning and Source of our existence, ages past.

We played that way, you know. A perfect harmony of love, trust, compassion, and forgiveness, compelling us to complete our own agreements, accomplish our own tasks, traversing a journey more sacred and solemn than what seems to exist between the melody and the rain; each note and every drop. Like the drops I feel rushing to the rhythm of my beating heart, this, and every moment I remain.

SUGGESTED READING

Life Lessons
   by Elisabeth Kubler-Ross and David Kessler

Lessons from the Light: What we can learn from the near-death experience
   by Kenneth Ring, Ph.D. and Evelyn Elsaesser Valarino

Closer To The Light: Learning from the near-death experiences of children; Amazing revelations of what it feels like to die
   by Melvin Morse, M.D, with Paul Perry

Destiny of Souls: New case studies of life between lives
   by Michael Newton, Ph.D.

Resilience From The Heart: The power to thrive in life's extremes
   by Gregg Braden, New York Times best-selling author of *The Divine Matrix*